PORTRAITS INDIA DRAWINGS &C.

PORTRAITS INDIA DRAWINGS &C.

A

CATALOGUE

OF A

GENUINE AND VALUABLE COLLECTION

OF

ENGLISH AND FOREIGN PORTRAITS

INDIA DRAWINGS &C

RICHARDSON

GYAN

Published by

Gyan Publishing House
5, Ansari Road
Daryaganj, New Delhi-110002
Phone: 011-47034999, 9811692060
E-mail: books@gyanbooks.com

Distribution Network
gyanbooks.com
India, USA, Canada, UK, Australia

ISBN: 978-93-7133-743-4 (PB)
First Published, 1799

2nd Impression 2025

Printed at: Gyan Press, Delhi.

PORTRAITS INDIA DRAWINGS &C.
Author Richardson

PORTRAITS, INDIA DRAWINGS, &c.

A

CATALOGUE

OF A

GENUINE AND VALUABLE COLLECTION

OF

ENGLISH AND FOREIGN PORTRAITS, INDIA DRAWINGS, &c.

COMPRISING THE CHOICEST WORKS OF

BARTOLOZZI, BLOOTELING, DELARAM, DREVET, ELSTRACK, FAITHORNE, HOGARTH, HOLLAR, LOGGAN, LOMBART, MASSON NANTUIEL, the PASSES, SHERWIN, SMITH, VERTUE, VANDYCKE, &c. &c. including ſeveral, rare and curious, of CHARLES the Firſt and Second, CROMWELLS, the ORANGE and PALATINE Families, &c. Among the Foreingers are many relating to Engliſh Hiſtory, particularly thoſe mentioned by BURNET, CLARENDON, GRANGER, &c. The Collection in general is in perfect Preſervation, and the fineſt Impreſſions;

WHICH WILL BE

SOLD BY AUCTION,

BY MR. RICHARDSON,

AT HIS HOUSE,

No. 31, the Corner of Villers-Street, in the Strand,

ON MONDAY, FEBRUARY 18, 1799,

AND THE EIGHTEEN FOLLOWING DAYS,

AT TWELVE O'CLOCK.

To be viewed three Days previous to the Sale. Catalogues, Price Three Shillings and Sixpence each, may be had of Mr. CLARKE, Bookſeller, Bond-ſtreet; Mr. GEO. COOPER, Glaſs-Manufacturer, No. 82, Lombard-ſtreet; and of Mr. RICHARDSON, No. 31, Strand.

‡†‡ MR. RICHARDSON begs to inform his Friends, that, in addition to his uſual Buſineſs, he propoſes ſelling Prints, Books, Coins, and every other Article intended for public Sale.

PRINTED BY T. BURTON, GATE-STREET, LINCOLN'S-INN FIELDS.

DAYS OF SALE.

FIRST DAY, -	*Monday*, -	*Feb.* 18	Foreign and Engliſh Portraits, A. & B.
Second Day, -	*Tueſday*, -	*Feb.* 19	B. Portraits continued, & Bartolozzi
Third Day, - -	*Wedneſday*,	*Feb.* 20	Foreign and Engliſh Portraits, C.
Fourth Day, -	*Thurſday*, -	*Feb.* 21	C. Portraits continued, RemarkableCharacters, and Portraits, D.
Fifth Day, - -	*Friday*, - -	*Feb.* 22	D. Portraits continued, Foreign & Engliſh, E.F.
Sixth Day - -	*Saturday*, -	*Feb.* 23	F. Portraits continued, Faithorne's Works, and Engliſh Portraits, G.
Seventh Day, -	*Monday*, -	*Feb.* 25	G. Portraits continued, Foreign & Engliſh, H. Hogarth, &c.
Eighth Day, -	*Tueſday*, -	*Feb.* 26	H. Portraits continued, & Hollar's Works
Ninth Day - -	*Wedneſday*,	*Feb.* 27	H. Portraits continued, Hiſtorical & Engliſh Portraits, I.
Tenth Day, - -	*Thurſday*, -	*Feb.* 28	I. Portraits continued, Jeſuits, Foreign & Engliſh Portraits, K. & L.

Eleventh Day,	*Friday*, - -	*Mar.* 1	Foreign and English Portraits, M. & N.
Twelfth Day -	*Saturday*, -	*Mar.* 2	—Ditto, N. O. & P.
Thirteenth Day,	*Monday*, -	*Mar.* 4	P. continued, Palatine Family, Politicals, Drawings, and English Portraits, Q. & R.
Fourteenth Day,	*Tuesday*, - -	*Mar.* 5	R. continued, & Portraits after Sir Joshua Reynolds
Fifteenth Day,	*Wednesday*,	*Mar.* 6	—R. continued, S. Portraits
Sixteenth Day,	*Thursday*, -	*Mar.* 7	—The Works of John Smith
Seventeenth Day,	*Friday*, - -	*Mar.* 8	Portraits S. and T. continued, Topographical, Portraits, V.
Eighteenth Day,	*Saturday*, -	*Mar.* 9	Portraits after Vandycke, and by Vertue
Nineteenth Day,	*Monday*, -	*Mar.* 10	Vertue continued, Portraits V. & W. Books of Prints, and Portfolios

Firſt Day's Sale.

FOREIGNERS.

A

1 TEN—Aretin, Arioſto, &c.

2 Three—F. Comte de Aſumar, Albert, Archduke of Auſtria, &c.

3 Five—L. M. D'Aumont, by Mallet—Agnes, Comteſe D'Arco, by Vermeulen—Marquis D'Argenſon, by Duflos, &c.

4 Nine—Popes Alexander the VIIth and VIIIth, various

5 Eight—Cardinals, &c.

6 Seven—Charles, Comte D'Auvergne, Fiquet, &c.

7 Two—Auguſtus III. King of Poland, and Queen, by G. F. Schmidt

8 Ten—anonymous—by C. Mellan, &c.

9 Eight—ditto—Poilly, &c.

10 Five —ditto—Boulanger, &c.

11 Five —ditto—Demarcenay, &c.

12 Seven—ditto—various

13 One—AUGEREAU, whole length, by P. M. Alix

ENGLISH MEZZOTINTO PORTRAITS.

A

14 One—James, Earl of Abercorn, after Gainſborough, 1778, whole length, by Dean

15 Three—Princeſs Anne and Amelia, grand-daughters to King George, by Lens; Princeſs Anne, by Becket; and Anne of Denmark, whole length, after Wiſſing, by J. Smith

16 Four—Princeſs Amelia, whole length, by Simon, 1728; Mary, Ducheſs of Ancaſter, whole length, by M'Ardell, *proof*; Elizabeth, Counteſs of Ancram, by V. Green, &c.

17 Four—three of the abdicated family; and Count D'Ada, by Becket

18 Three—Mr. Allen, of Bath, by Faber, 1754; Henry Angelo, by B. F. Scott; and the Honourable James Anneſly, by A. Miller

19 Five—Count D'Ada, by Becket; J. Forteſcue Aland, by Faber, 1733; Addiſon, ſold by Smith; Dr. Arne, by Dunkerton, *proof*

20 Four—John, Duke of Argyll, by J. Simon

21 Three—ditto, whole length, by J. Faber, 1740; John Armſtrong, 1742, by M'Ardell; and the Hon. Thomas Burnet, by Faber

22 Seven—anonymous, &c.

ENGLISH ENGRAVED PORTRAITS.

A

23 Thirteen anonymous

24 Four—the abdicated family, by Chereau, &c.

25 Four—ditto, by J. G. Will, 1748, F. V. Schuppen, 1692, &c.

26 Three—ditto, Maria Clementina, with a crucifix, by Roſſi; Louiſa Maria, fol. by Chereau; and one by C. Dupuis

27 Three—ditto, Clementina, by Jac Freij; one ditto, by P. Drevet, &c.

28 Four—Anſon, by Houbraken—the ſix admirals, by Bickham; the admirals, by Ravenet; and Athlone, by Haelweg

29 Five—Athlone, by R. White; the ſix admirals, by Bickham—the Hon James Anneſley, by ditto; Major André, by J. K. Sherwin, &c.

30 Four—Guſtavus Adolphus, by Delff; Duke of Albemarle, by Gammon; ditto, by Davis, &c.

31 Eight—Duke of Albemarle, &c.

32 Six—Earl of Aileſbury, by White; the Earl of Arundel and Alathea Talbot, &c.

33 Two—Earl of Aileſbury, by White; and one called the Earl of Arundel, by Voſterman—ſee Granges, vol. 2. page 112

34 Three—John Anthony, M. D. by Croſs—John Archer, M. D. and William Auſtin, by Glover—*very fine and ſcarce*

35 Nine—Ann of Denmark, by Houbraken; Ann of Cleeve, by ditto, &c.

36 Seven—Guſtavus Adolphus; Francis D'Andrada, Portugueſe miniſter; Duc D'Alva, &c. &c.

37 Nine—Cornelius Agrippa, &c.

38 Three—The Earl of Albemarle, by Gaywood; Aſhburnham, by Davis; and Sir Edward Aſtley, by Worlidge

39 Three—Addey, by Sturt; two of John Ayres, by White, quarto and octavo; and one ditto, by Sturt—*all fine*

40 Two—Abraham Aurelius, RARE; and William Auſtin, by Glover

41 One—GUSTAVUS ADOLPHUS, on horſeback, with a view of Lypzig, and an engagement, by Jacob Heyden, 1632—FINE AND RARE

42 One—ditto, allegorical, with German inſcriptions, 1632—VERY CURIOUS

43 One—EARL OF AILESBURY, by Harrewyn—VERY RARE

44 One—Chriſtopher, DUKE OF ALBEMARLE, by W. Sherwin—FINE AND RARE

45 One—George, DUKE OF ALBEMARLE, by LOGGAN, 1661—EXTRA FINE AND RARE

46 Two—Albert, and Iſabella of Auſtria, by John Eillarts, in ſuperb dreſſes—*ſcarce*

47 One—SIR THOMAS ALLAN, of Suffolk, by Vanderbanc—*very fine and ſcarce*

48 One—ARCHIBALD, EARL OF ARGYLE, with armorial bearings, by Vanderbanc—FINE AND RARE.

49 One—Archibald, Earl of Argyle, by D. Loggan—*fine*

50 Two—Sir John Aſtley, by Worlidge, on ſattin—and JOHN ASHTON, by R. White—BOTH PROOFS, RARE

51 One—SIR WILLIAM ASHURST, Lord Mayor, 1694, by R. White—RARE

52 Mr. Juſtice Aſhurſt, by J. Jones, 1796

53 Nine—Atkins, the gout doctor, and Sir John Aſtley, by Worlidge, &c.

CLERGY.

54 Six—Richard Alleſtry, by Loggan; Hen. Aldrich, by Heath, &c.

55 Six—Biſhops, Andrews, of Wincheſter, &c. by Payne, 1641; ditto, by Paſs, 1618; Rob. Abbot, of Saliſbury, by F. Delaram; F. Atterbury, by M. V. Gucht, &c.

56 Three—Richard Alleſtry, by D. Loggan; L. Andrews, by Vaughan; and Thomas Attwood, 1643, by W. Marſhall—*fine*

57 One—Henry Airay, Provoſt of Queen's College, from a monumental plate—*ſcarce*

58 One—Father Archangelus, 1631 — *very fine and rare*

FOREIGN PORTRAITS.

B

59 Ten—Ducheſſe of Burgundy, &c.

60 Four—Bayle, J. B. Boyer, &c.

61 Ten—Boileau, Balſac, &c.

62 Five—J. B. de Blye, G. Edelinck, &c

63 Thirteen—Cardinal Barberini, Bellarmain, &c.

64 Seven Lud. Comte de Brienne, and Vondoſme, Duc de Beaufort, by Nantuiel, &c.

65 Six—Dukes of Burgundy, by Suyderhoef, &c.

66 Three—Charles, Duke of Brunſwick, by D. Marcenay, &c.

67 Seven—Fred. Will. Margrave of Brandenburgh, of Brandenburgh, on horſeback; Charles, Duc de Bourbon, &c.

ENGLISH ENGRAVED PORTRAITS.

B.

68 Seven—Blakeney, Sir John Barnard; Children of Wilbraham Bootle, &c.

69 Nine—Francis Bugg, quarto, by V. Hove; Walter Blith, Blanchard, Brooks, W. M. &c.

70 Five—Earl of Bath, by Martin, 1763; ditto, *a proof*; Sir Robert Boyd, by Hall, 1789; one ditto, by Caroline Watron; Colonel Barry, by Nutter, 1789

71 Seven—Lud. Cappellus, Ferd. Duke of Brunſwick, by Houbraken, 1777; Burſenſki, Poliſh Miniſter—*rare*; A. G. Buſbequius, &c.

72 Two—Bidloo, *proof*, by Bloteling; and one other

73 Two—Sir James Bland Burges, by P. W. Tomkins, 1796; Horace Beckford, *proof*, by Condé, 1792

74 The Right Hon. Iſaac Barre, by John Hall, 1787

75 Four—Horace Beckford, by Condé; Lant. Brown, by J. K. Sherwin; Dr. Wm. Boyce, by ditto, 1775; and Yngr Burge, Eſq.

76 Three—Walter Baker, by Worlidge; Gab. Briſcoe, by W. Sherwin, 1709; and Thomas Brodrick, by ditto, 1704—*all fine*

77 Three—Sir Samuel Barnardiſton, by White, 1700; Sir John Blencowe, by W. Sherwin; and Henry, Viſcount Bolingbroke, by Deſrochers

78 Fifteen—Buchanan, Sir Thomas Browne, octavo, John Browne, R. White, Sir Robert Berkeley, by Powle, &c.

79 Seven—Viſcount Falconbergh, by R. White, &c.

80 Five—Oldenbarnevelt, quarto, Henry Blacwood, by Mellan—John Barclay, Peter Bortius, and Baudius

81 Eight—Sir F. Bacon, Lord Burleigh, by Houbraken; Capt. Bedloe, quarto; John Brown, by White, folio; ditto, quarto, and Ann Bullen

82 Five—Thomas Brugis, by Crofs; Sir Francis Bacon, William Barriff, Richard Brathwait, by Vaughan; and John Brown, by Gaywood—*all fine*

83 Four—Sir F. Bacon, by Marfhall; Barriff in armour, quarto; Sir Robert Berkeley, by Powle; and Richard Brownlowe, by Crofs—*fine*

84 One—Lord Burleigh, from the Bifhop's Bible

85 WILLIAM BLUCK, by R. White—FINE AND RARE

86 Three—Chriftian, Duke of Brunfwick, by Queboren, 1623; one ditto, by S. Pafs, with hat and feather; and George William, Duke of Brunfwick, by De Jode

87 Eleven—Portraits to illuftrate Granger

88 Nine—Thanes Autographs, &c.

89 Two—Poets—BARON, by Marfhall; and RICHARD BROOME, by Crofs—BOTH RARE

90 Two—JOHN BABINGTON, by Droufhout; and JOHN BATES, by G. Giffard, FINE AND RARE

91 One—ALDERMAN BACKWELL, old impreffion, VERY SCARCE

92 Two—WILLIAM BARRIFF, by Glover; and one with ornaments æt. 42—FINE AND SCARCE

93 Two—Oldenbarnevelt, folio; and Bidloo, by A. Blooteling

94 Two—Lord James Beauclerc; and Charles, Earl of Burford, fons of Eleanor Gwin, by ditto—*fcarce*

95 One—MARY, DUCHESS OF BEAUFORT, by J. Nutting, before the insertion of "DOWAGER"—VERY FINE AND RARE

96 One—LUCY HARRINGTON, COUNTESS OF BEDFORD, by SIMON PASS—RARE

97 One—ANN BILL, by ditto, THE ORIGINAL PRINT—*very rare*

98 One—MARTIN BILLINGSLEY, the writing master, by W. Hole—FINE AND RARE

99 One—Sir HENRY BLOUNT, the traveller, by D. Loggan, 1679—VERY FINE AND RARE

100 One—JOHN DIGBY, EARL OF BRISTOL, with staff of chamberlaine, sold by W. Peake—VERY RARE AND FINE—From the Fothergill collection

101 Sir William Brog, 1635, Crispin Van Queboren—*fine and rare*

102 One—ROBERT, LORD BROOKE, by G. VALCK, 1678—FINE AND RARE

103 Two—RICHARD, LORD BUCKHURST, by S. Pass, VERY RARE; and the copy

104 One—George, Duke of Buckingham, folio, by Delff *fine and scarce*

105 One—George, Marquis of Buckingham, by J. K. Sherwin, 1788—*proof*

Second Day's Sale.

FOREIGN PORTRAITS.

B

1 FOUR—Broglio, Lieutenant General, by Vermeulin; Marquise de Beringhen, by Roullet; Duc de Beaufort, by Nantueil; and Charles, Comte Buquoy, by Sadeler

2 Ten—Cardinal Barberino, Baromée, &c.

3 Eight—Artists—Seb. Bourdon, &c.

4 One—CARDINAL BOSSUET, by Drevet—*fine*

5 One—ditto

6 One—SAMUEL BERNARD, by ditto—*the first impression*

7 One—GELLIUS DE BOUMA, by C. VISSCHER—*fine*

8 One—Buonaparte on horseback, by J. J. Tassaert

9 One—Berthier, whole length—*mez.*

10 One—Charles de Belleisle, by Will, 1743

C

ENGLISH PORTRAITS.

MEZZOTINTO CLERGY.

A to B

11 Two—Biſhop Atterbury, 1718, by J. Simon, and Thomas Baker, by ditto—*proof*

12 Four—Baker, by Simon; Rad. Battell, by ditto; Biſhop Berkeley, by Brooke; and Thomas Birch, by Faber, 1741

13 Two—the ſeven biſhops, by J. Gole; and ditto by R. Robinſon—*ſcarce*

14 Five—Birch, by Faber; Thomas Burnet, by ditto, 1752; Thomas Bradbury, Robert Bragge, by Faber, 1738; and Thomas Brett, 1743, by M'Ardel

15 Two—Hugh Boulter, by J. Brooks, whole length; and Richard Buſby, 1695, by James Watſon

16 One—Daniel Burges, æt. 61, 1707, in an oval, by J. Faber—*very rare*

BY F. BARTOLOZZI.

17 Two—Veſtris, in a large circle, and a Sunday concert

18 One—The tranſparency at Sir Joſeph Banks's, on the recovery of the King, 1789, after W. Hamilton—*fine proof*

19 One—the inſide view of the Royal Exchange; the etching—*ſcarce*

20 One—Vandyck's wife and child—AN AQUAFORTIS PROOF; RARE

21 One—Maria, Archducheſs of Auſtria, ſiſter to the late Queen of France, after Roſlin, 1782—*proof*

22 Five—Addiſon, *proof*; D'Ageno, after Gainſborough; Antoinette, Queen of France; G. A. Bellamy; and Lady Berkeley—*proof*

23 One—Charles, Earl of Camden, after Gainſborough

24 Two—Catherine, Empreſs of Ruſſia, whole length, 1785—*one an unfiniſhed proof—curious*

25 Two—ditto, *an unfiniſhed proof*; and Lady Duncannon, after Downman

26 One—LADY CATHCART — PROOF *before the border, rare*

27 Four—Princeſs Amelia, after Lawrence; Lady Cheſterfield, with an urn; Maria Coſway; and Anne, Counteſs Cowper

28 One—William, Duke of Clarence, whole length, after Weſt—*proof, ſcarce*

29 Three—Lord Cornwallis, ſmall oval, *proof*; Captain Cooke, ditto; and the Earl of Chatham's monument

30 Three—Leonard Euler, *proof*; Foſter, Speaker of the Commons in Ireland, ditto; and Lord Fitzgibbon, after Coſway, ditto

31 Two—Lady Elizabeth Foſter, after Sir Joſhua; and Mrs. Gautherot

32 One—Miſs Farren, after T. Lawrence—*fine proof*

33 One—Guy's monument—*ſcarce*

34 Two—Count Gertzie, and Lord Hawke—*proofs before any writing, very ſcarce*

35 One—Lord Heathfield—*proof*

36 Two—Gertrude, Marchioneſs of Hallifax—*one a proof before the plate was made leſs, ſcarce*

37 Two—Joſeph Haydn, and Henderſon — *proofs before name of engraver, &c.*

38 Two—Henry the VIth, and Henry Chichele, founders—*ſcarce*

39 Four—F. Ruſſell, Earl of Bedford; Th. Eliott; Lord Cobham; and Lady Richmond; from the Court of Henry the VIIIth

40 Four—John Leak, M. D. *proof*; Mrs. Lenox, Mrs. Montagu, and E. Malone

41 One—Mary, Queen of Scots, whole length, after Zuchen—*proof*

42 One—the Duke of Newcaſtle, Colonel Litchfield, &c. return from ſhooting, after Wheatly—*proof*

43 One—Marquis Peſſari, the Venetian reſident—*proof*

44 One—the Hon. William Pitt, after Gainſborough Dupont

45 One—Mary, Sophia, and Amelia (Princeſſes) after Copley

46 One—Miſs Emily Pott, as "Thais," after Sir Joſhua Reynolds—*proof*

47 Four—Mrs. Montagu; Philidor; ditto, *a proof*; and Maſs Pinellius

48 Two—Lieutenant J. G. Riddell, and Colonel Stanley—*private plates*

49 One—Sir George Saville, from his monument

*49 A ditto

50 Three—Princeſs Sophia; and two of Jane Shore, different

51 Two—Margaret Rudd; and the Ducheſs of Rutland—*proof*, *ſcarce*

52 Three—Thomas Ruddiman, æt. 75; Ignatius Sancho; and Henry Swinburne—*proofs*

53 Three—the Prince and Princeſs of Wales; Dr. Willis; and Theobald Wolfe—*ſcarce*

54 Three—girl with pidgeons, Maria, &c. by Ryland—*proofs*

55 One—the exhibition at the Royal Academy, 1789, with portraits of their Majesties, by Martini—*proof*

56 Two—the happy and deserted village, by J. K. Shirwin—*proofs*

ENGLISH ENGRAVED PORTRAITS
CONTINUED.

CLERGY.
B

57 Eleven—Francis Bugg, by Van Houe; Joshua Barnes, by G. White; Thomas Burnet, by B. Wilson, 1751, &c.

58 Twelve—Baxter, Ezekias Burton, by R. White; Bolton, by Payne, 1602, &c.

59 Seven—Isaac Barrow, octavo, by W. Bates; the seven bishops, &c.

60 Three—Joseph Beaumont, by R. White; Thomas Becon, wood cut profile, 1553; and John Bunyan, by Sturt, folio

61 Seven—Bishop Thomas Barlow, of Lincoln, by R. White; Cardinal Beaufort, William Beveridge, of St. Asaph, octavo, Baynbridge, John Bridgeman, of Chester, 1623, by Trotter; Gilbert Burnet, by Picart; and the seven bishops, by A. Haelweg

62 Five—Baxter, folio, by R. White; W. Bridg, 1670, by William Sherwin, Brightman, æt. 45, Bolton, by Payne, 1632; and Robert Burton, by le Blon, 1638

63 One—ISAAC BARROW, by D. LOGGAN, folio—*proof*, FINE AND RARE.

64 One—RALPH BATHURST, by D. LOGGAN, folio, 1676—*proof*, FINE AND RARE

65 One—James Bentham, of Ely, after T. Kerrich, by Facius, 1792—*proof*

66 Three—the seven bishops, by Haelweg; ditto, by D. Loggan; and Bishop Burnet, by M. Vander Giest—*fine*

67 One—Michael Boyle, Bishop of Armagh, by D. Loggan—*fine and scarce*

68 Two—William Burkit, by R. White, 1703; Thomas Burnet, by B. Wilson, 1751

69 Two—Richard Busby, 1695, by R. White; and Henry Burton, by G. Glover

ENGLISH MEZZOTINTO PORTRAITS.

B

70 Two—the Hon. George Baillie, of Jerriswood, 1719, by V. Hacken; and Mr. William Barker, by Faber, 1726—*scarce*

71 One—James, Earl of Barrymore, by Ford—EXTRA RARE, NOT IN BROMLEY

72 Four—John Barber, Lord Mayor, 1733, by Faber, 1740; Arthur Beardmore, by James Watson; Alderman Benn, by Fabar; ditto, by M'Ardall

73 One—Alderman Benn's club, by Faber

74 One—Admiral William Bartley, by R. Tompson—*scarce*

75 One—William Bates, Esq. æt. 78, by V. Green—*proof*

76 Three—Pulteney, Earl of Bath, by Simon; William, Duke of Bedford, 1700, by R. Williams; and Richard, Earl of Burlington

77 One—Mark Beaufoy, 1781, after Gainſborough, by V. Green—*private plate*

78 Four—John Banniſter, by R. Williams; John Baptiſte, by G. White; H. Beverland, by J. Becket; and Elizabeth, Counteſs of Bridgewater, by Simon

79 Three—William Beckford, Lord Mayor; ditto, with Townſend and Sawbridge, by R. Houſton; and Julian Beckford, Eſq. by ditto, with maſquerade dreſs—*proof, before feathers in the hat*—*ſcarce*

80 Four—Madam Barré, by T. Watſon; Lady M. C. Bertie, by J. Dixon, 1767, *private plate*; Louiſa, Counteſs Berkeley, by Faber, 1742; and Elizabeth, Counteſs of Bridgewater, by Simon

81 Four—Madam Baker, by Becket; Lady Bellaſis, by R. Tompſon; Lady Bradſhaigh, by Faber, 1744; and the Counteſs of Bridgewater, by Simon

82 Two—Beverland and his wife, by Schenck; and one of Monſ. Beverland in an oval, by W. Sherwin—*ſcarce*

83 One—Beverland and his wife, by J. Becket—*fine*

84 Three—Admiral Belcher, by Faber, 1734; Boſcawen, 1747, by ditto; and the Hon. Charles Brown, by ditto, 1740

85 Four—Hon. John Beresford, by Hodges; Cadwallader, Lord Blayney; Henry Boyle, by I. Brooke, 1742, whole length; and the Hon. William Brownlow, by C. H. Hodges

86 Three—Mrs. Billington, by Dunkerton—*ſcarce*; Miſs Brown, by V. Green; and Miſs Bruſby, by ditto

87 Three—Mr. Blakes, by M'Ardell; a ditto, firſt impreſſion, before this man, &c. was introduced; and Jack Briſtowe, by Faber, 1746

88 Two—Mr. John Boydell, by V. Green—*proof*; and William Browne, 1765, by J. Dixon

89 Three—John Boydell, by V. Green; James Brindley, by Dunkerton, 1773; and J. Bryer, by V. Green—*proofs*

90 One—Lord Bridport, by V. Green

91 One—George, Duke of Buckingham, by Becket, *proof*—SCARCE

92 One—Edmund Burke, by J. Jones, *proof*

93 Four—Sir Richard Blackmore, by G. White; Boyle; Butler, *a proof*; and the Hon. Thomas Burnet, by Faber

94 Three—Admiral Bofcawen, whole length, by M'Ardel; Byng, 1757, by Houfton; and Sir George Byng, by Faber, 1718

95 One—Admiral Blake, by Thomas Prefton—*fine*

Third Day's Sale.

FOREIGNERS.

C

1 NINE—Prince de Condé, &c.

2 Nine—Gilbert de Choiſeul, &c.

3 Five—Thomas Corneille, by Thomaſſin, &c.

4 Five—Clement, Prince of Baviere, by J. Andran; J. B. Coignard, by Petit; M. de Charmois, by Simoneau, &c. &c.

5 Seven—Charles II. King of Spain, by Richard Collin; Charles III. by R. White, &c.

6 Nine—Charles XII. King of Sweden, by R. White; Chriſtiana, Queen of Sweden, &c.

7 Five—Catherine, Empreſs of Ruſſia, &c.

8 Six—Cardinal Camus, by Thomaſſin. &c.

9 Seven—Popes, Clement VIII. X. XI. XII. XIV. &c.

10 Five—Artiſts, Coypel, &c.

11 Eleven—ditto, Carracci, Corregio, &c.

12 One—ADRIENNE LE COUVREUR, by Drevet—*fine*

D

13 One—CATHERINE DE BOURBON, IN A SUPERB DRESS, by John Wierx—*fine*

14 Eighteen—the National Convention

15 Thirty-two—ditto

16 Eighteen—ditto

17 Fourteen—nobility, generals, &c.—*in colours*

ENGLISH ENGRAVED PORTRAITS.

C

18 Six—William Cockburn, M. D. by White; William Cookſon, by ditto; Miſs Carew, by Lovelace, &c.

19 Seven—Cortes, by Vertue; Earl of Clarendon, Lord Coventry, Richard Cromwell, &c. by Harding

20 Nine—Culpeper, James Cooke, by R. White; William Cole, by ditto, &c.

21 Seven—Campen, by Suyderhoef; Duc de Choiſeul, Caſſini, Charles Crequi, &c.

22 Three—Chardin, by Loggan; Sir Robert Cotton, folio, by R. White, 1696; and John Cockſhuit, by Loggan

23 One—JAMES CALTHORPE—FINE AND RARE

24 Five—James Cats, Peter Collins, by C. Galle—*fine*; Phil. de Comines, Cluſius, and Capellus

25 Three—Sir Ewen Cameron, *rare*; Earl of Carliſle, by A. Bloteling; and William, Earl of Craven

26 One—SIR HUGH CARTWRIGHT, by L. Vorſterman—VERY RARE AND FINE

27 Two—Queen Catherine, by N. Bylls, *ſcarce*; and Charles II. by P. Weillamſon—*fine and ſcarce*

28 One—QUEEN CATHERINE, by Adrian Lommelin—VERY RARE AND FINE

29 One—Queen Catherine, with her coat of arms; cupids, &c. by P. WEILLAMSON—*very fine and rare*

30 Two—Queen Catherine, whole length, by Ed. Davis; and Charles II. in armour, folio, by V. Dalen—*both fine*

31 One—ditto, whole length, as St. Catherine, by W. Sherwin—*ſcarce*

32 Four—Charles I. with the cap in his hands, preparing for execution, &c.

33 Nine—various, of Charles I. and II.

34 Two—Charles I. and Henrietta Maria, after Vandyke, by de Jode—*fine*

35 One—CHARLES I. OLIVER CROMWELL, and GENERAL FAIRFAX, in three ovals—VERY RARE

36 Two—Charles, and Henrietta Maria, by Delff—*fine*

37 One—Charles I. ſitting in his robes, ſceptre, &c. by W. Paſs—VERY RARE AND FINE

38 One—ditto ON HORSEBACK, M. de St. Antoine holding his helmet, by P. Lombart—FINE AND RARE

39 One—ditto, ſlaſhed dreſs, hat and feathers; view of the ſea, by H. DAVID—VERY RARE AND FINE

40 Three—Charles ON THE SCAFFOLD, label from his mouth, giving a paper to the executioner; ditto, with a globe, by Marſhall

41 One—ditto, LYING IN STATE—VERY RARE AND CURIOUS

42 One—Charles I. in an octagon, between FAIRFAX AND CROMWELL; a lion and fox; army in the back ground—VERY RARE

43 One—CHARLES I. and his QUEEN playing at Cards with the DUKE of BUCKINGHAM, &c. after Vos, by Alexander Voet—FINE AND RARE

44 One—ditto, after ditto, Jaſper Iſaac *executit*.

45 One—Charles I. taking the triple crown from the Pope, backgammon board and money on the table; on the left are the Kings of Sweden and Denmark, COUNT GONDAMOR, &c.—CURIOUS AND RARE

46 One—Charles the Firſt, ſitting in parliament, nineteen portraits of nobles, &c.—*very rare*

47 One—CHARLES THE FIRST, SITTING IN PARLIAMENT, NOBLES, &c. WITH A COMPLETE BORDER OF THEIR COATS OF ARMS; ON THE TOP IS A GENEALOGICAL TREE, WITH PORTRAITS OF HENRY VII. AND VIII. EDWARD VI. ELIZABETH, EARL OF LENOX, MARY QUEEN OF SCOTS, JAMES I. AND CHARLES I. IN OVALS, WITH THEIR EMBLAZONMENTS—MOST RARE AND CURIOUS

48 Seven—various, of Charles I. and II.

49 Five—ditto, one on vellum

50 Six —ditto, ditto

51 Ten—ditto

52 Six —ditto, the biſhops crowning the king, ſmall oval; Charles II. on horſeback, with Mrs. Lane, &c.

53 Three—Charles II. whole length, in robes, ſhips at a diſtance; ditto, in a ſquare of oaken foliage, by J. Chantry; ditto, ſtanding on a monſter—*fine*

54 Three—Ditto, one by R. Maſon; ditto, with Mrs. Lane; and one in THE OAK TREE—FINE AND RARE

55 One—ditto, IN AN OVAL, by Danckers—FINE AND RARE

56 One—ditto, ditto, by R. Gaywood—*ditto*

57 One—ditto, whole length, in armour, on the right is the ſeven-headed monſter, under him the head of Charles I. the death-warrant, and in the back ground

is the execution of Charles I. &c. &c.—*most rare and curious*

58 One—Charles II. and his Queen, with the royal family and Dukes of the royal blood, the Archbishop of Canterbury and the clergy presenting an address—*rare and curious*

59 One—Charles II. on horseback, in armour, crown on his head, view of Windsor-castle, by P. Stent—*rare and curious*

60 Three—the entertainment of Charles II. and his Queen at the Hague

61 Three—Charles II. by L. Spirinx, 1664; a ditto, by Bouttats; and Oliver Cromwell, by Gunst.

62 Three—Charles V. a circle, æt. 57, 1557; a ditto, by Suyderhoef; and one after Titian

63 One—CHARLES V. WITH HIS GREAT DOG, by Visscher—*curious*

64 Four—Charles V. by Lombart, &c.; and Christian V. King of Denmark, by de Jode, 1650

65 Two—Charles V. with emblems; and Charles XI. of Sweden—*proof*

66 One—EARL OF CHATHAM, PROOF, by J. K. Sherwin

67 Two—CHARLES CHAUNCY, by Caroline Watson; and NATHANIEL CHAUNCY, by Nutter—BOTH PROOFS, ON INDIA PAPER—RARE

68 Four—Lord Cobham, by Bickham; Lord Carteret, by Major; Earl of Chatham, by Barry; and Lord Carleton, by Houbraken.

69 Six—Sir William Cornwallis, by T. Cecill; Robert, Earl of Castlemain, &c. &c.

70 Three—Richard Collins, by Browne, 1676; Thomas Cross, senior in his school, *rare*; and Henry Coley, 1668—*fine*

71 Six—William Chamberlain, by Hertochs; Culpeper, by Crofs, &c.

72 Seven—P. Collinfon, Cuming, Cleghorn, D. Clare, &c.

73 Six—Robert Cotton, folio, by White, 1696; Sir Edward Coke, George Croke, &c.

74 One—Chriftian IV. King of Denmark, by Muller, 1625—*very fine*

75 One—ditto, with his fon Frederic, whole lengths, by William Pafs—*fine old impreffion*

76 Two—one ditto; and Charles V. by C. Galle

77 Two—EDWARD COCKER, writing mafter, by Gaywood—FINE AND RARE

78 Two—Odet Coligni, with his brothers; and Gafpar, Count Coligni, by Delff, 1631

79 One—Contareno, the Venetian minifter, by Vorfterman—*fcarce*

80 One—Sir Thomas Coventry, lord keeper of the great feal—*rare*

81 Two—Oliver Cromwell in armour, the head of Charles, and others laying on each fide of him; and Charles II. by Vanderfteen

82 One—Oliver in a carr, drawn by monfters, drove by the Devil, under the wheels is Charles I. &c.—*rare and curious*

83 Four—Cromwell, by Picart; one as head of the fanaticks, by Bickham; the etching of ditto; and one ftanding in armour, with the royal oak

84 Seven—various; Oliver and Richard Cromwell, by Harding

85 One—Cromwell on horfeback, by Lombart—*fine*

86 One—DITTO, WITH HAT AND FEATHER, VIEW OF LONDON—*a ſheet, very fine and rare*—F. Mazot, *excudit.*

87 One—CROMWELL, by VANDEVELDE, O. C. P. R. AT THE CORNERS—FINE AND RARE

88 One—ditto, THE MEDALLION, the French and Spaniſh ambaſſadors diſputing—*ſcarce*

89 One—ditto, in armour, page putting on his ſaſh, by Gaywood—*fine and rare*

90 Two—Cromwell, in his right hand the Axe, and in his left the head of Charles; and the execution of Charles, oval, by Peter Huybrecht—*very rare*

91 One—ditto, with the triple crown, a Scotchman under his foot, an Iriſhman between his legs, a Frenchman under his arm, and embowelling a Dutchman with his right hand; in the back, execution of Charles I. &c.—*very rare*

92 One—ditto, diſſolving the Parliament; "begone you rogues you have ſate long enough;" "*this houſe to let*"—*very rare and curious*

93 One—ditto, monkey with triple crown on his head, lion aſleep in a cradle, &c. &c.—*very curious*

94 One—DITTO, IN THE PULPIT PREACHING, SEVERAL MALE AND FEMALE SPECTATORS—RARE AND CURIOUS

95 Two—ditto, in armour, ſword in his left hand and ſaſh on ditto, fleet and army in the back ground; and Richard Cromwell, ditto, in oval, by Sturt; before the words "late Protector" was added—*both fine and rare*

96 Five—Richard Cromwell, in armour, ſquare—*fine*; ditto, by Harding; Joan Cromwell; Charles II. with

crown and fceptre, æt. 1660, fleet in the back ground, large quarto, fold by Sturt, &c.

97 One—Edward Chifenhale, of Chifenhale—*very fcarce*

98 Five—William, Duke of Cumberland, on horfeback, by Baron; and John, Earl of Crawford, by Worlidge

99 Four—Capt. Cook—*proof*, by Holloway; Duke of Cumberland, by Ravenet; John, Earl of Crawford—*proof*, by Worlidge; and Sir Roger Curtis, by J. Caldwall, 1783

100 Five—George, Earl of Cumberland; Arthur, Lord Chicher Thane; Charles, Earl of Carlifle, by A. Bloteling, &c.

101 Ten—portraits to illuftrate Granger

102 Fifteen—Thanes autographs, &c.

Fourth Day's Sale.

ENGLISH ENGRAVED PORTRAITS CONTINUED.

CLERGY.

C

1 SEVEN—Le Cene, by M. La Cave; T. Cockman, Richard Conyers, L. L. D. Dr. Cooke, by Harding; &c. &c.

2 Seven—Cranmer, Richard Challoner, Richard Corbet, by Harding, &c.

3 Four—Cortes, by Dunſtall; Joſeph Caryl, folio, by R. White; Steph. Charnock, by ditto; and Comenius, by G. Glover—*fine*

4 Six—Canynges, by Jenner; Clarke, by Dunſtall; ditto, by Binneman, &c.

5 Five—Joſ. Caryl, by White; Comenius, by Croſs; Clarke, by Gaywood, 1654; Coſin, by W. Dolle; and Sam. Craddock, by R. White

6 Two—Henry Compton, Bishop of London, by D. Loggan, 1679; and Walter Carle, 1647, by T. Cecill—*scarce*

MEZZOTINTO CLERGY.

7 Four—Robert Camell, L. L. D. Christ. Clarke, by Faber, 1740; Matthew Clarke, by G. White; and Alured Clarke, Dean of Exeter, by Wills

8 Three—Christ. Clarke, by Faber; Dr. Cooper, after Copley, by V. Green; and Francis Couplet, the Chinese, by Faber, whole length, 1736

9 One—Bishop Crew, by F. Place—*fine and rare*

10 Two—Bishops—Carmichael, 1753, by J. Dixon; and Clavering, by Simon—*scarce*

11 Three—ditto — Chicheley, a founder; Compton, by Becket; and Crewe, by J. Faber, 1727

12 Five—John Cennick, by Dawe; T. Clarkson, by J. Young; Dr. Dodd, &c.

REMARKABLE CHARACTERS.

13 Twenty-three—anonymous, &c.

14 Five—Old Aldridge; Æsop of Eton, in an oval; Jack Adams, &c.

15 One—Jacob Bates, the famous English horse-rider, by Nusbiegel, 1766—*scarce*

16 Eight—John Barefoot; James Bick, of Oxford, 1712; Edward Burrell, of Norwich, 1629; John Bexley, Jed. Buxton, &c.

17 Three—Broughton, with seven verses; Edw. Bright; Jed. Buxton, by Spilsbury

18 Nine—Mrs. Brownrigg, the etching by Dance; Miſs Blandy, by Ryley, &c.

19 Two—Thomas Britton, the muſical ſmall-coal man, eight Engliſh verſes, by J. Simon; a ditto, tuning an inſtrument, by Thomas Johnſon, with eight verſes—*ſcarce*

20 Eleven—Baithes, Thos. Browne of Yorkſhire, Blanchard, John Brading, &c.

21 Two—COLONEL BLOOD, by G. WHITE, with THE ETCHING—RARE

22 Seven—Elizabeth Canning, and George Collingwood, executed at Liverpool, 1716, &c.

23 Twelve—George Carpenter, godſon to King George I.; Duncan Campbell; Matthew Champion, aged 108; Thomas Coryate, the traveller, 1616, &c.

24 Six—Bamfylde Moore Carew, by J. Faber, 1750; Miſs Chudley; Thos. Collins, by Warren; Will. Crouch, by Pelham, &c.

25 Twelve—William Dewell, by M. La Cave, 1740; Dugdale, Drybutter, &c.

26 Seven—Morgan Davis, by Chapman; Richard Dickenſon; John Dean, the only ſurvivor of the ſixteen men which remained on board the ſhip Suſſex, 1741, by J. Faber, &c.

27 Three—John Elwes, Eſq.; Henry Evan, æt. 104. *mez. in oval*, 1710, &c.

28 One—EVA FELIGEN, THAT LIVED IN CLEVELAND WITHOUT FOOD, ÆT. 40, with ſix Engliſh verſes; ſold by G. Humble—*ſcarce*

29 Seven—William Fuller, æt. 32, 1670, H. Flleet, æt. 104, 1761, by W. Dickenſon; Frederic Forreſt; Margaret Finch, Queen of the Gipſies, 1739, &c.

30 Two—Mother George, æt. 120, by B. Lens; and William Groves, grand maſter of the rolls, by P. R. Fremont, 1734; ſix Engliſh verſes—*rare*

31 Eight—John Guttwen; Bernard Gigli, a giant, by J. Fougeron, Granny, &c.

32 Four—John Gale; Richard Gaſcoign, executed 1716; Joſeph Gerrald, by J. W. Reynolds; and John Hanna, executed 1739

33 Three—Humphreys, the boxer, by J. Young—*proof*; Boxing-Match, between ditto and Mendoza, by Grozier; and Daniel Mendoza, by W. N. Gordenir.

34 Three—Hardman, the corn-cutter, by W. Wilſon—*proof*; Nicolas Hart, the ſleepy man, born in Holland, 1648; and Hobſon, the carrier, 1690, by J. Payne, eight Engliſh verſes—*ſcarce*

35 Five—John Hall, executed 1716; Matthew Henderſon, by J. Grimſton, 1746; John Hanna, &c.

36 Ten—J. Hall, Job Hart, Capt. Hooke, &c.

37 One—JACOB HALL, ROPE-DANCER, THE ORIGINAL, by de Brune—FINE AND SCARCE

38 Two—Hamet Ben Hamet, and John Potemkin, ambaſſadors, 1682, by R. White—*very fine*

39 Four—H. Jenkins, æt. 169, a mez. a ditto, by Worlidge—*fine*; Jemmy, the Scotch Piper, ſix verſes

40 One—Job, ſon of Sollimon—*ſcarce*

41 Seven—Iſaac Ingall, æt. 118, by Yeatherd; John Gale Jones, Benjamin Jarrat, &c.

42 Seven—Indian Chiefs brought from Carolina, by Sir Alexander Coming, 1730, *ſcarce*

43 Four others, by Simon

44 Six—Viſcount Kenmure, executed 1716; Kilmarnock and Balmerino, 1746; Sally King, Moll King, Ed-

ward King, with Abel Roper, with emblem of pillory and gallows, &c.

45 Three—MOTHER LOUSE, OF LOUSE-HALL, THE ORIGINAL PRINT—*rare and two copies*

46 Ten—Wybrant Lolkes, in London, 1791; J. Lee, æt. 103, 1728, by W. Goldfinch; M'Leane, 1750; Lebeck, by Miller, 1739

47 Nine—John Molesworth, the calculator; Sir Edmund Mason, &c.

48 Five—Anna Macallame; Harry Morgan, æt. 105, 1737; Maddox, the wire-dancer, by R. Houston; and Michael de Molinos, &c.

49 One—JAMES NAYLOR, BY F. PLACE, EXTRA RARE, from the Fothergill Collection

50 Six—James Nayler, four English verses; John Napier, by J. Lodge, &c.

51 Four—Margaret Patten, æt. 136, 1739; Mrs. Sarah Porter, by Smithson; Miss Pond, by Spilsbury; and Peter, the wild boy, by V. Green—*proof*

52 Four—Hugh Peters, delivering a petition, by W. Sherwin; a ditto, a mez. where Father Peters is riding on a lobster, &c.—*rare and curious*

53 Four—Richard Penderill, by R. Houston; Sir Richard Perrot, by V. Green; John Philips, of Yorkshire, æt. 117, 1742, by J. Faber; and John Pixley, of Ipswich, by ditto, 1749

54 Eight—Old Parr, æt. 152, by G. White; Young Parr, by ditto; Penderill, Prance, &c.

55 Twelve—William Parsons, Robert Powell, &c.

56 Four—Charles Ratcliffe; Henry Rogers, pewterer of Cornwall; Caroline Rudd, by Sibelius, &c.

57 Seven—John Reeder, Sessarakoo, by J. Faber, 1749; Riqua, a Chinese, by Burford, 1757, &c.

58 Four—Jack Sheppard, by G. White; James Sheppard, a mez. in an oval, by Faber; and one ditto, an etching, executed 1718—*ſcarce*

59 Seven—Martha Saunders, æt. 104, 1775; Edward Scofield, æt. 71, *proof*; Jane Scrimſhaw, æt. 126, 1710, by Faber; a ditto, æt. 127, 1711; Mary Smith, by Worlidge; a ditto, by M'Ardel; and Hannah Snell, by Johnſon

60 Nine—Dick Swift; Old Scarlet, the ſexton of Peterborough, æt. 98, 1594; Henry Simons, &c.

61 Six—Mrs. Sage, by Burke—*a proof*; Old Scarlet; Mr. Skeggs; Edward Scofield, æt. 71, &c.

62 Eight—Grace Toſier, &c.

63 One—Barbara Urſlerin, the original—*ſcarce*

64 One—Ditto, mez. folio, with Latin and Engliſh deſcription—*ſcarce*

65 Five—William Walker, æt. 123, 1736, by G. Bockman; Little Will; John Worley, pentioner, by Faber, 1709; Thomas Wood, &c.

66 Eight—Iſobel Walker, æt. 112, 1774; John Woolderidge, of Eaſt Clanden; Woodhouſe, &c.

ENGLISH MEZZOTINTO PORTRAITS.

C

67 Three—Charles, Lord Camden, whole length, by Spilſbury, 1766; Philip Cheſterfield, ditto, by Brooks; and Robert, Lord Clive, by M'Ardel

68 Two—William, Lord Cadogan, by Simon; and Geo. Lord Carpenter, by Faber

69 Three—Charles, Earl of Carliſle, by Faber, 1732; Sir Eyre Coote; and William, Lord Craven, by Faber, 1745

70 Six—Callaghan, Captain Chriſtian, Joſ. Champion, &c.

71 One—John Carr, architect, by C. H. Hodges—*private plate*

72 Five—Duc de Choiſeul, 1770, by Lowry; Charles of Lorraine; Henry Clarke, by Faber, &c.

73 Two—Lord Charlemont, whole length; and Arthur O'Connor, by. W. Ward

74 Two—W. B. Conyngham, by V. Green, *proof*; and Sir Samuel Cooke, lord mayor of Dublin

75 Six—Queen Catherine, by Bloteling, 1680; Charles II. by ditto; ditto by Vandervart; Charles I. by W. Faithorne; ditto, ſold by Smith; and Oliver Cromwell, ſmall oval, O. C.

76 Three—Charles I. after Vandyke, by Becket; Chas. II. by Williams; and one ditto, whole length, ſitting in his robes

77 Four—the Hon. Charles Cecil, by Lens, *a proof*; Elizabeth, Counteſs of Cheſterfield, by Becket; Ducheſs of Cleveland, by ditto, ſitting; ditto, in an oval

78 Three—Caroline, Princeſs of Hanover, by W. Faithorne; the Ducheſs of Cleveland, ſitting, bracelet on her right arm, by E. Lutterell; a ditto, half ſheet, by Alexander Browne

79 Four—Queen Catherine, by Bloteling, 1680; Counteſs of Clarendon, by Beard; Miſs Cooper, by Faithorne; and Maria, Counteſs of Coventry, by R. Houſton

80 One—MRS. DOROTHY CRESSY, by R. Williams—SCARCE

81 One—ROBERT CONY, M.D. by E. Luttrell, 1707—SCARCE

82 One—OLIVER CROMWELL, LORD PROTECTOR; and JOHN LAMBERT, Lieutenant General; by A. Miller, 1745—VERY RARE, *a ſheet*

83 Five—Queen Caroline, by Fabar, 1739; Princeſs ditto, 1728, by Simon: Queen Charlotte, by V. Green—*proof*; and two of Maria, Counteſs Czerniehew

84 Three—Miſs Cabben, Mrs. Clarke, and Maria Coſway, by V. Green—*proofs*

85 Three—Chriſtian VII. King of Denmark, by Fiſher: and Caroline Matilda, Queen of ditto, by Watſon, &c.—*proofs*

86 Four—Jenny Cameron, by Johnſon; Mrs. Chelſum, æt. 87, 1789, by Pether; Anne, Counteſs of Cork, by James Watſon, *proof*, &c.

87 Two—William, Duke of Clarence, by V. Green, *proof*; and the children of Frederic, Prince of Wales, by Faber

88 Two—Francis Seymour Conway; and Richard Cumberland, by V. Green—*proofs*

89 Three—Miſs Catley, by Dunkerton, *proof*; Mr. Chalmers, in Midas, by Watſon; and Mrs. Clive, by Faber, 1734

90 One—Mrs. Cibber, in the character of Cordelia, by P. van Bleeck, 1755, before the plate was reduced.

91 Four—Joannes Careſtini, by Faber, 1735; Harry Carey, by ditto; Colley Cibber, by Fiſher, 1758; and William Drummond, by Finlayſon.

92 Three—Joſeph Carreras, by Faber, 1735; William Cadogan, M. D. 1769, by Dickenſon; and Dr. Cullen, by V. Green—*proof*

93 Four—Edward, Earl of Clarendon, by Johnſon; Sir John Coke, by G. White; Sir Robert Clayton, Lord-Mayor, 1680, by J. Smith; and Braſs Croſby

94 One—The Ducheſs of Cumberland, whole length, by V. Green—PROOF

95 One—Allegorical to the memory of Lady Elizabeth Cutts; Lord Cutts on one ſide of the print, and on the other is armour, deſigned by Tate, poet-lauret, B. Lens fecit—*a ſheet, very rare and curious*

96 One—The Monument of William, Earl of Chatham, by V. Green—*proof*—*large ſheet*

97 One—Queen Charlotte and the Princeſs Royal, after Weſt, by V. Green—*proof*

98 One—The Royal Children, after ditto, by ditto

ENGLISH ENGRAVED PORTRAITS.

D

99 Six—William Deſeſch, by M. le Cave, 1751; Andrew Duncan, M. D. Trotter; George Dyer, by Elizabeth Criſtall, &c.

100 Five—Sir Hew Dalrymple, by R. Cooper; Hew Dalrymple, by A. Bell, &c.

101 Four—Captain Dampier, by J. K. Sherwin; Andrew M'Dowall, *proof*, by Worlidge; Princeſs Daſchkaw, by Scorodomoff and George Dyer

102 Two—Thomas Denman, M. D. by Skelton, 1792; and the Right Hon. Sylveſter Douglas, *proof*, by E. Harding, 1794

103 Six—Marquis D'Angeau, *proof*, by P. Drevet; Douſa; Druſius, &c.

104 Four—Admiral Drake, Sir Hew Dalrymple, by Cooper, &c.

105 Four—The Counteſs of Dorcheſter at confeſſion, and the Counteſs of Derby, by Gardiner, &c.

106 Three—James, Earl of Derby, by Loggan, *ſcarce*; John Day; and Admiral Drake

107 Two—Thomas, Earl of Danby, by A. Bloteling; and Sir Edward Deering, by Glover—*fine*

108 Three—Dalton, by W. Marſhall; ditto, by Tyſon; and John Day

Fifth Day's Sale.

FOREIGNERS.

D

1 SIX—Admiral Van Dorp, &c.

2 Four—Cardinal Dubois, by DREVET; J. D'Eſtrees, by AUDRAN; G. Daillon Du Lude, by N. Pitau, &c.

ENGLISH MEZZOTINTO PORTRAITS.

D

3 Four—Madam Davis, by Thompſon; Counteſs of Derby, quarto, by Williams; Charles, Earl of Derby, by Bloteling; and John, Earl of Exeter, by Thompſon

4 Two—Louis Dejean, Eſq. by Faber; and William, Lord Digby, 1743, by ditto—*ſcarce*

5 Three—Sir Francis Dashwood, by Faber, 1753; Arthur Dobbs, by M'Ardell; and Francis Douce, M. D. æt. 75, by ditto, in an oval

6 Two—Sir Thomas Dennison; and Robert Dingley, Esq.—*proofs*, *scarce*

7 Four—Flora M'Donald; Peter Dore—*proofs*; Francis Douce, on horseback, æt. 75, by M'Ardell; and William Draper, of Yorkshire, by J. Faber

8 One—Georgiana, Dutchess of Devonshire, after Maria Cosway, whole length, by V. Green—*proof*

9 Five—William, Duke of Devonshire, by Faber, 1733; ditto, whole length, by Brooks; Charles, Earl of Dorset, by Smith; ditto, by Simon; and Lionel, Duke of Dorset, by M'Ardell, 1750

10 Two—Baron Dimsdale, by Burke; and Christopher de Dreyer, by J. Jones—*private plate*—*scarce*

11 One—The Hon. Archibald Douglas, by V. Green—*proof*

12 One—Admiral Sir Charles Douglas, whole length, by J. Jones

13 One—Mr. Robert and Mr. Thomas Drummond, ditto, by V. Green—*proof*

14 One—Henry, Earl of Danby, after Vandyck, by ditto

15 Two—James Daillon, Comt du Lude, 1693, by P. Pelham; and Sir John Dolben, Preband of Durham, 1750, by J. Faber—*scarce*

ENGLISH ENGRAVED PORTRAITS

CONTINUED.

16 Six—Descartes, Countess of Derby, &c.

17 Two—William Daviſſon, by P. Lombart; and Rupert Douglas, by Falck, 1651

18 One—GEORGE, VISCOUNT DARTMOUTH, by P. Vandrebanc, with trophies, ſheet—VERY FINE AND RARE

19 One—WILLIAM, EARL OF DENBIGH, by Voerſt—*fine and ſcarce*

20 One—ditto, ditto

21 Three—SIR WILLIAM DICK, of Braid, EXHIBITING HIM IN PROSPERITY, PRISON, AND DEATH, by R. and W. Vaughan—VERY FINE AND RARE.

22 One—William Dobſon, etched by himſelf—*fine and rare—from the Fothergill collection*

23 One—Dr. Doriſlaus, ſtanding with a maſk in his right hand, three ditto hanging on his left arm; Time, Truth, and other curious hiſtorical emblems—*very rare*

24 One—Admiral Drake, with a globe ſuſpended under an arch—*the original print—fine old impreſſion.*

25 Twelve—Portraits to illuſtrate Granger, Autographs, by Thane, &c.

CLERGY.

26 Eight—Doddridge, by G. Vertue, 1751; John Dolben; Theodore Dorrington, by Bouttat; Ducke, by J. Clarke; Dunſter, &c.

27 Four—Sir William Dawes, by Gribelin; John Dallaeus, by Lombart, 1670; Durant, 1650, &c.

FOREIGNERS.

E

28 Six—J. L. Duc D'Efpernou, by M. Lafne; G. D. Ehrot, by Haid, mez. Leon Euler, by Steenglin, mez. Charlotte D'Efmares, by Lepicie, &c.

29 One—ELIZABETH OF BOURBON, by H. WIERIX—*firſt impreſſion—rare and fine*

ENGLISH MEZZOTINTO PORTRAITS.

E

30 Two—Admiral Edwards, by Dickenfon; and Capt. Farmer—*proofs*

31 Four—John, Earl of Egmont, by Faber, 1734: Charles Erfkine, by M'Ardel—*proof*; Thomas Erfkine, by James Walker; and Sir Robert Eyre, J. Cooper, exe.

52 Four—Edward VI. by Pether—*proof*; Elizabeth, Queen of Edward IV. by Faber; Princefs Elizabeth, whole length, ditto, &c.

33 Three—Mary, Countefs of Effex, by Faber; Lady Erfkine, by Watfon; and Prince Eugene, by Simon

34 One—John Ellicott, clock-maker to his Majefty, by Dunkerton

35 One—Lord Chief Juftice Eyre, by V. Green

36 One—Mr. Deputy Ellis, æt. 83, by W. Pether—*proof—ſcarce*

ENGLISH ENGRAVED PORTRAITS.

E

37 Five—The murder of Edward the martyr, at Corfe Caſtle, by Cazali—*print and proof*; three of prince Edward—by Dalton

38 Four—Prince Eugene in armour—*ſheet*; one ditto on horſeback, ſold by Collins, &c.

39 Twelve—Kings and Queens of England, from Hume, &c.

40 Eight—ditto—by Paſſe, &c.

41 Six—Richard Elton, by Drouſhout; Earl of Eſſex, by W. Marſhall, &c.

42 Six—Clement Edmonds, Richard Elton, by Drouſhout, &c.

43 One—ADELBERTUS EGGUIS, by J. V. Velde—VERY FINE AND RARE

44 Six—Elizabeth, &c.

45 One—ditto, Henry Hondius, 1632—*fine and rare*

46 Four—ditto—one by Anton Wierix; one ditto, emblematical, *curious*; and three others

47 One—DITTO, WHOLE LENGTH, IN THE SUPERB DRESS SHE WENT TO ST. PAUL'S TO RETURN THANKS FOR THE DEFEAT OF THE SPANISH ARMADA, *a beautiful impreſſion* after Iſaac Oliver, by Criſpan Paſſe—*very rare*

48 One—ROBERT, EARL OF ESSEX, IN HAT AND FEATHER—I. P.

49 One—DITTO, ON HORSEBACK, IN ARMOUR, HAT AND FEATHER, ARMY AND FLEET IN THE DISTANCE, 1601—EXTRA FINE AND RARE

50 One—Thomas Cromwell, Earl of Eſſex, by Filian, from the Fothergill collection—*fine*

51 Two—Chevalier Eſtriene, by Langot; and the copy

52 Two—Bern Duc D'Eſpernon, by V. Schuppen, 1661; one ditto, by Nantuil—*both very fine*

53 Twelve—Sir Thomas Erpingham, by Thane, &c.

CLERGY.

54 Two—Eraſmus, after Holbein, by C. Koning—*fine*; and one from his ſtatue, with a view of Rotterdam, by D. Stoopendael

55 Five—Eraſmus, by J. Hopfer, quarto; ditto, whole length, octavo, by W. Marſhall; Dr. Everard; Matt. Earbery, by Cole, &c.

56 Four—Clement Ellis, æt. 68, W. Evats, by T. Croſs; John Everard, by ditto; and Eraſmus, quarto, Stent, exe.

FOREIGNERS.

F

57 Six—FAGELUIS, by Tanje; L. U. Le Fevre, by Vermeulen, &c.

58 Four—Ferdinand I. by Soutman; one by Hondius; Ferdinand III. by Suyderhoef; and another by J. Sandrart

59 Seven—Frederick, King of Pruſſia, by Haas; one ditto, by Houbraken; one ditto, by Gunſt, &c.

60 Three—ADMIRAL FLORIST, Count Fontaine, by L. Vorſterman; and Count Fuenſaldana, by ditto

61 Seven—Cardinal de Fleury, by Chereau; F. J. Fleury, by Duchange, &c.

62 Four—Artifts, La Fage, by Vermeulen; Jac Frey, mez. by Haid; Charles de la Foffe, by Duchange, &c.

63 Five—Leonardus Fofcolo, by Picini, &c.

G

64 Six—Pope Gregory XIII. by Jac Frey, &c.

65 Eight—Duc de Gesures, whole length, by Petit; Peter Gillet, by Drevet, &c. &c.

66 Eight—Marquis de Gefures, by Morin; Henry, Duc de Guife, by ditto, Admiral Van Galen, by Mewzyn, &c.

ENGLISH MEZZOTINTO PORTRAITS.

F

67 Four—Sir John Fielding, by M'Ardell; Lord Henry Fitzgerald, by T. Park; the Hon. Duncan Forbes, by Faber, 1748; and the Hon. William Fortefcue, by ditto, 1741

68 Two—Robert Fielding, with a dog, one altered

69 Two—ditto, one in armour, by Beckett—*proofs*

70 One—Sir John Fielding, after Peters, by W. Dickenfon—*fine*

71 Two—the Hon. Mary Fielding, by Beckett; and Lady Fortefcue, by Watfon—*proof*

72 Two—Mr. Fielder, Fruit Broker, and Dr. Fothergill, by V. Green—*proofs*

73 One—John, Lord Fitzgibbon, by Hodges, whole length—*proof*

G

74 One—Right Hon. John Foster, ditto, ditto

75 Three—William Fittock, Mayor of St. Maws, Cornwall, 1741; Richard Ford, of Chertsey, 1774, by E. W. A.; and Treg. Frampton, Esq. æt. 87, 1728, by Faber

76 One—the Hon. Charles James Fox, from the Bust, by Pether

77 Four—Francis, Emperor of Germany, by Faber, 1745; Frederick, King of Prussia, by W. Faithorne; Frederick, Prince of Wales, by Simon; and Mrs. Faber, by Faber

78 Four—Frederick, King of Prussia, by W. Sherwin; ditto, by G. Valch, &c.

79 One—Sir Stephen Fox, 1701, by Simon

80 Four—Benjamin Franklin, 1761, by M'Ardell; Mr. Frye, Dr. Fothergill, by V. Green—*proofs*; and Francis Ferguson, by Haward

CLERGY.

81 Three—John Edwards, by J. Watson; Sir George Fleming, Bishop of Carlisle, by J. Faber; and James Foster, by V. Bleeck

ENGLISH ENGRAVED PORTRAITS.

F

82 Four—Jacob, Lord Folkstone, by Charles Sherwin, *private plate*; Lady Charlotte Finch, by Major, *ditto*; Colonel Fanning, by Reading, *ditto*; and Benjamin Franklin, by Heath

83 Six—Capt. Forreſt, by Sharp, 1779; Colonel Fanning, George Faulkner, by Sharp, 1777, &c.

84 Five—Farrinelli, by Wagner; Fleming, by Hibbert; Jonathan Fentum, by Collyer; Frodſham, &c.

85 Two—Miſs Farren, by Collyer; and Lady Elizabeth Foſter, by Caroline Watſon

86 Four—Lady Lettice Falkland, by Marſhall; Lord Falkland, by V. Gucht, &c.

87 Seven—Lord Fairfax, by Worlidge; Viſcount Fauconberg, Lord Finch, &c.

88 Six—Thomas Fidell, by Croſs; Thomas Flatman, by R. White; N. C. Fabricus, by Mellan, &c.

89 Three—Frederic William, King of Pruſſia, by J. Gole, &c.

90 One—GENERAL WILLIAM FAIRFAX, ſix verſes—*very fine and rare*

91 Three—Sir Thomas Fairfax, on horſeback, by W. Marſhall; a ditto, by Worlidge, ſmall oval; and one ditto, inſcribed "*fare fac*"—*ſcarce*

92 One—Thomas, Lord Fairfax, with Dutch verſes, by Savry—*fine and ſcarce*

93 Two—one ditto, in armour, in an oval rich border; Huych Allardt, in ditto, a ſquare, octavo

94 One—THOMAS, VISCOUNT FAUCONBERG, by A. Bloteling, 1676—*ſcarce*

95 One—Sir John Fenwick, by R. White—VERY RARE

96 One—Ferdinand, Duke of Brunſwick—PROOF, FINE AND RARE

97 Two—Francis I. by S. Perjecouter, 1536—*ſcarce and curious*; a ditto, by Morrin

98 One—ditto, by Auguſtin, the Venetian, 1536—RARE AND CURIOUS

99 Three—Frederic William, Elector of Pruſſia, by Cornelius Viſſcher, 1649; a ditto, Prince, by J. Swelinck; and Frederic William, by E. Deſcrochers, folio

100 One—Frederic III. of Denmark, on horſeback, piſtol in his right hand, by H. Allardt—RARE AND CURIOUS

101 Three—Frederic II. King of Pruſſia, by WILLE; Frederic, Prince of Wales, by B. Baron, 1753, &c.

Sixth Day's Sale.

ENGLISH ENGRAVED PORTRAITS
CONTINUED.

CLERGY.

F

1 SEVEN—Richard Farmer, by Ridley, 1791; Wm. Friend, D. D. by T. Worlidge; Mr. Friend, by Birrell; Benjamin Francis, by Trotter; James Foſter, by Ravenet, &c.

2 Six—William Falkner, by Sturt; D. Featly, by W. Marſhall, 1645; Henry Finch, folio, John Flavell, 1680, by R. White; and William Fulke, 12mo. two verſes

3 Six—the five biſhops; Robert Farrar, &c. by R. White; a ditto, ſold by Overton, &c.

4 Four—Daniel Featly on the tomb, John Flavell, 1680, by R. White; Mark Franck, by W. Dolle; and William Fulke, æt. 50, by W. Marſhall, fol.—*fine*

By FAITHORNE.

5 One—Edmund Anderſon, æt. 76—*fine*

6 Two—Robert Bayfield, 1654, with the hat; one ditto, æt. 27, in a cap—*fine and rare*

7 One—Sir Orlando Bridgeman—*fine*

8 Three—Edward Boys, æt. 66; Lane Bolton; and Ralph Brownrig, æt. 67, 1659, four Engliſh verſes

9 One—Ralph Brownrig, ditto; and one ditto, octavo—*very fine*

10 One—John Bulwer—*proof*—*rare*

11 One—Catharine, Queen of Charles II. in the dreſs in which ſhe came to England

12 One—DITTO—CAPITAL

13 Two—Charles, Earl of Carliſle; and Charles I. in armour, in an oval

14 One—Charles I. in armour, front face, in an oval, ſold by Peake—*fine*

15 One—Prince Charles, front face, in a large oval, after William Dobſon—*very fine*

16 One—Charles II. face a three-quarter turned to the left, in armour, ſaſh, the George hanging under the right arm, in an oval—*fine proof*—*very rare*

17 One—Henry, Lord Colerane, ſitting and writing, as a pilgrim, Jacob's ladder and other emblems—*ſcarce*

18 One—Samuel Collins, M. D.—*fine*

19 Two—Sir William Davenant and Queen Elizabeth, ſitting; Lord Burleigh and Sir Francis Walſingham, ſtanding on each ſide

20 One—Edmund Ellis, æt. 28, 1662, in an octagon—*—very rare*

21 One—Robert, Earl of Effex, after Dobfon, in the manner of Mellan—*fine and very rare*

22 One—FRANCES BRIDGES, DOWAGER COUNTESS OF EXETER, AFTER VANDYCK—VERY RARE AND FINE

23 One—SIR THOMAS FARFAX—ditto, ditto

24 One—Sir Richard Fanfhaw—ditto

25 Two—one ditto, and Elizabeth, with Lord Burleigh and Sir F. Walfingham

26 One—Jof. Glanvill—*fine*

27 One—Henry, Duke of Glocefter, æt. 20, 1660, in an oval, P. Stent, exc.

28 Two—Anton le Grand; and Sir Bevill Granvil, æt. 39, 1640—*fine*

29 One—Valentine Greatrakes—*fcarce*

30 Two—John Hacket, æt. 68, 1670, four verfes—one a *proof*—*very rare*

31 One—James, Marquis Hamilton, after Vandyck—*fine*

32 Two—Sir James Harrington, æt. 45, 1654, in an octagon; and John Kerfy, after Souft, 1672

33 One—Henrietta Maria, Queen of King Charles I. in a religious habit, in the manner of Mellan—*rare*

34 One—*ditto*—*fine proof, ditto*

35 One—Henry, Earl of Holland, in an oval; fold by Robert Peake—*fine and rare*

36 Two—Richard Hooker, in an oval, fupported by two globes; and John Hacket, folio

37 One—THOMAS KILLEGREW, Page to King Charles I. 1650, after W. Sheppard—VERY FINE AND RARE

38 One—ditto, ditto

39 One—Edward, Lord Littleton—*fine*

40 One—Edward, Lord Littleton—*fine*

41 Two—Robert Loveday, in an octagon—*very fine*; and Henry, Earl of Monmouth

42 One—Thomas Mace, æt. 63, after H. Cooke—*very fine*

43 Two—Henry More, fitting under a tree—*very fine*; and Francis More

44 One—Henry Cary, Earl of Monmouth, ditto

45 One—George Viscount Mordaunt, with armorial bearings, ditto

46 Two—Morton, Bishop of Chester; and John Murcot, æt. 30, 1654, six English verses, ditto

47 Two—Bishop Morton; and Francis Moore, ditto

48 One—Sir John Ogle, ditto

49 Two—William, Prince of Orange, in a Vandyck dress, sold by Peake; and Mary, Princess of ditto, sold by William Faithorne

50 One—Mary, Princess of Orange, ditto

51 One—ditto, sold by Robert Peake, ditto

52 One—William Oughtread, ditto

53 One—SIR WILLIAM PASTOU, 1659

N. B. This is esteemed Faithorne's finest portrait---*extra rare*

54 One—John Pordage—EXTRA FINE

55 Two—Bishop Prideaux, and Christopher Simpson, in ovals—*fine*

56 One—CAREW REYNELL, from the Forthergill collection—EXTRA FINE AND RARE

57 One—James, Duke of Richmond, after Vandyck, ditto, ditto

58 One—ditto

59 One—Francis Rous, æt. 77, 1656, four English verses; and a copy on India paper—*scarce*

60 One—Prince Rupert, front face, and ſaſh, in an oval, after Dobſon, ſold by Thos. Rawlett—EXTRA FINE AND RARE

61 One—ditto, ſold by Stent

62 One—DITTO, IN ARMOUR, RIGHT HAND ON THE BREAST, AFTER VANDYCK, *ſold by Robert Peake*—EXTRA RARE AND FINE

63 One—Maria Ruten, after ditto—*rare*

64 One—Thomas Stanley, in an octagon, after P. Lilly—*fine*

65 One—ditto

66 One—MARGARET SMITH, AFTER VANDYCK—*very fine and rare*

67 Three—William Sanderſon, æt. 68; Chriſtopher Simpſon, quarto, after J. Carwarden; and Thevenot, whole length—*fine*

68 One—Dr. Jeremy Taylor, ſtanding on a pedeſtal—*proof before the quotations*; *fine and rare*

69 One—Robert, Earl of Warwick, ſold by William Peake—*fine and rare*

70 One—ditto, *ditto*

71 One—George Rodolph Weckerlin, after Myſens—*fine and rare*

72 One—Bulſtrode Whitelock—*fine and rare*

73 One—James, Duke of York, front face, in armour, ſaſh over the left ſhoulder, in an oval—*fine proof*, *very rare*

74 Twenty-two—Kings and Queens of England, from William the Conqueror to Elizabeth—*very fine*

*74 Ten—James I. and Queen; Charles and Henrietta Maria; William, Prince of Orange, and Princeſs Mary; Fred. Henry, and Princeſs Amelia, &c.—*very rare*

ENGLISH MEZZOTINTO PORTRAITS.

G

75 One—Garrick leaning on the buſt of Shakſpeare, after Gainſborough, by V. Green—*proof*

76 One—Garrick and Mrs. Pritchard in Macbeth, after Zoffani, by V. Green—*proof*

77 One—Garrick in Abel Drugger, after ditto, by Dixon —*proof*

78 Three—Henry Gale, of Taunton Dean, 1742, by J. Faber; Richard Gomeldon, by W. Faithorne; and Samuel Greathead, Eſq. by Houſton—*ſcarce*

79 Three—Mr. Gay, by F. Kyte; Thomas Gent, by V. Green, *proof*; and Aretin George, by Faber, 1738

80 Four—Baptiſt, Earl of Gainſborough, by Faber; Henry, Earl of Galway, by Simon; Luke Gardnir, Eſq. by J. Brooks; and Admiral Griffin, by Houſton

81 One—George III. Queen and family, after Zoffany, by Earlom—*proof, ſcarce*

82 One—George II. whole length, by Dickenſon—*fine*

83 Three—George, Prince of Denmark, by Williams; a ditto, by Faithorne; and a ditto, Becket *exc.*

84 Three—George, Duke of Hanover, born 1666, ſold by Cooper; King George; the Prince and Princeſs of Wales, by Simon; and George II. on his throne, by T. Ryley

85 One—Lord George Germain, after Romney, by Jacobé—*fine proof*

86 Two—Baron Ginkel; Earl of Athlone, by P. Schench, quarto; and one by Williams, folio—*ſcarce and fine*

87 Two—James Gibbs, by Pelham; and George Graham, clock-maker, by Faber

88 One—Valentine Green, 1788—*fine*

89 One—Sir Henry Gould, by T. Hardy

90 Three—Henry, Duke of Grafton, whole length, in his robes, by Becket; a ditto, in a ſmall oval, E. Cooper, *excud.*; and Iſabella, Ducheſs of Grafton, whole length, by Lens

91 One—Duke of Grafton—*proof*

92 Two—Henry, Duke of Grafton, quarto, in an oval, by Becket; and one with a dog—*proof*

93 Two—the Duke and Ducheſs of Grafton, in ovals, by P. Schenck—*ſcarc*

94 One—Auguſtus Henry, Duke of Grafton, 1762, by James Watſon—*ſcarce*

95 One—Lady Charlotte Greville, by J. Young—*proof*

96 Four—George II. after Worlidge, *proof*; George, Prince of Wales, and Prince Frederick, by Watſon; Frederick, Prince of Wales, by Pether; and the Hon. Geo. Grenville, by Houſton

97 Two—Geminiani, and Morgan Graves, by Val. Green —*proofs*

98 One—Griffin and Johnſon, by Van Bleeck, 1748—*ſcarce*

99 One—Mrs. Mary Grimſton, by J. Becket—*ſcarce*

Seventh Day's Sale.

ENGLISH MEZZOTINTO PORTRAITS

CONTINUED.

G

1 THREE—MaryGrimſtone, by J. Gole; Ellen Gwynn, by Van Bleeck, 1751; and Madam Graham, by Thompſon

2 Two—Joſeph Gulſton, Eſq. by James Watſon; and Mrs. Gulſton, by Earlom—*proof*

3 One—Joſeph and John Gulſton, after Coates, by Val. Green—*proof*

4 Two—John Gunning, profile in a circle, 1760; and the three Miſs Gunnings, in one plate, by Houſton—*rare*

5 One—the three Miſs Gunnings, by ditto; with the poem on gratitude, by John Gunning, 1756—*very rare*

6 Two—Henry Grattan, Eſq. and Lieut. Griffiths, by Val. Green—*proofs*

7 Three—Comtesse de Genlis, by ditto; Lady Grammont, by M'Ardel; and Madame Grovestins

8 One—Henry Gyles the glass-painter, of York, by Place *fine and scarce*

CLERGY.

9 Two—Garnett, Bishop of Ferns, 1752, by M'Ardel; and Thomas Gooch, of Ely, 1749, by ditto—*fine*

10 Four—Edmund Gibson, of London, by P. Pelham, 1724; S. Glass, small quarto; Thomas Gooch, by M'Ardel; and John Guise, by Faber, 1734

ENGLISH ENGRAVED PORTRAITS.

G

11 Nine—Garrick, in Tancred, by Worlidge; a ditto, by J. Wood, 1745; Serjeant Glynn, Gibbon, by Hall, &c. &c.

12 One—Garrick at the bust of Shakspeare, after E. Pine, by Caroline Watson—*a sheet*

13 Eight—Lady Jane Gray, &c.

14 Three—Ambrose Godfrey, 1738, by G. Vandergucht; Roger Grant, oculist; and Foote Gower, by Skelton

15 One—JOHN GURNEY, of Norwich, 1719, in an oval, sheep feeding, ships sailing, &c.—RARE

16 Five—Capt. ——— Grose, an etching; Thos. Gurney, short-hand writer, by Collyer; W. Grant, Esq. by J. R. Smith; and Count Gandie and Wife, by D. Berger, 1788; and Edw. Gibbon, by Hall

17 Three—Thomas Gale, æt. 56, *wood cut*; John Gerarde, the herballist, by W. Rogers, and one from the title page—SCARCE

18 One—JOHN GAMBLE, by T. Cross—VERY RARE

19 Six—George I. by Chereau, jun.; Sidney Godolphin, and Baron de Goertz, &c.

20 Four—George I. by G. W. Monguibert, 1733—*scarce* &c. &c.

21 Two—George II. and III. on horseback, by R. Ravenet; and Peter Mazell

22 One—George III. by W. W. Ryland, whole length, 1769

23 One—RICHARD GETHINGE, æt. 32, by J. Chantry—FINE AND RARE

24 Three—Sir Edmondbury Godfrey, by P. Vandrebanc, folio, &c.

25 One—ditto, by ditto—*large sheet, fine*

26 Two—Henry, Duke of Gloucester, by C. Van Dalen, *fine*; a ditto, by Moncornet

27 Two—Jaqueline, Duchess of Gloucester, and her husband, by Folkema, 1753

28 Two—George, Prince of Wales, by Sharp, 1790; and Sir Charles Grey, by Collyer, 1797

29 Two—Thomas Greene, original and copy

30 Two—Eleanor Gwynn, an etching, with a flower in her hair, from the Fothergill collection; and Jaqueline, Duchess of Gloucester, after Van Eyck

31 Three—Madam Gwin, with a nosegay; a ditto, with a lamb, by Ogborne; and an etching of ditto

32 One—Eleanor Gwynn, sitting, a flower in her left hand—*fine and rare*

33 Ten—Sir Harbottle Grimstone, Sir Thomas Gargrave, &c. Thane

*33 Eleven—portraits to Granger, &c.

34 Three—Count Gondomar, whole length; Duc de Gramont; Edelinck; and J. George, Duke of Saxony, 1652, by C. Waumans

35 One—COUNT GONDOMAR, in an oval, by Simon Paſſe, 1622—VERY FINE AND RARE

36 Three—Goldſmith, by Croſs, RARE; John Gadbury, by ditto; and James Gouter, by Livins

37 Three—Garencieres, by W. Dolle; Fran. Gomarus, æt. 45, 1609; and Hugh Grotius, by W. Delff

38 Four—P. Gaſſendus, Mellan, Ferd. Gonzaga, Grynæus, and Rud. Gualtherus, by C. Meyer

CLERGY.

39 Seven—John Gill, Crad. Glaſcott, Sir Adam Gordon, by C. Knight; Granger, Griffiths, by Fittler, &c.

40 Eight—Biſhop Gauden, by Croſs, &c.

41 Two—James Gardiner, Biſhop of Lincoln, by G. White, 1653; and B. Giffard, by Du Boſe—*fine*

42 Two—John Goodwin, windmill over his head, "error" and "pride" blowing the ſails, ſixteen Engliſh verſes—*very rare*; and a ditto, æt. 47, 1641, by G. Glover

43 Four—Biſhop Gauden, by T. Croſs, 1653; a ditto, by Paul; John Goad, 1689, by R. White, twelve Latin verſes; and Thomas Goodwin, 1679, by R. White, fol.

44 One—Dionyſius Grenville, æt. 54, by G. F. Edelinck, 1693—*very fine and rare*

FOREIGNERS.

H

45 Three—ADMIRAL VAN HULST, by Jan. Viſſcher; Count Horn, by FALCK; and Nicholas de Harley, by Meellen

46 Three—Admiral Van Hulſt, by Viſcher; COUNT HERBERSDORFF, on horſeback, by Lucas Killian, 1625; and JOHN HOUERBEEKE, by J. FALCK—FINE

47 Eight—Pope Hadrian VI. by Houbraken; H. L. Hobert de Montmor, by Mellan; one ditto, by Pitau, &c.

48 Six—Bart. Vander Helſt, mez. by A. Bloteling; John Hallius, by W. Delff, &c.

49 One—Hoche, whole length, mez. Coqueret

ENGLISH ENGRAVED PORTRAITS

CONTINUED.

H

50 Seven—Robert Hall, by Trotter; R. Henry, by J. Caldwall; Rowland Hill, by Collyer; Leon. Howard, by Golder; L. Howel, by J. Fellows; H. Hody, by M. V. Gucht, &c.

51 Nine—Joſ. Hall, C. Hickman, by Gribelin; Ez. Hopkins, by Sturt, &c.

52 Six—John Hart, D. D. Thomas Heather; P. Heylin, by R. White; J. Hewit, Thomas Hyde, by Perry, &c.

53 Two—Bishop Hall, by Payne, fol. eight verses; and Cardinal Howard, by Noblin—*fine and scarce*

54 Two—John Hewitt, six verses; Robert Henderson, with curious emblems, by M. Droushout, 1632

55 Three—Henry Hibbert, by D. Loggan, six verses; Arthur Hildershaun; and Hez. Holland—*fine and scarce*

ENGLISH MEZZOTINTO PORTRAITS.

H

56 Five—Admiral Hawke, Haddock, by Faber; Sir Charles Hardy—*a proof*; Richard, Lord Howe, by James Watson; and Sir Thomas Hardy, by Faber, 1722

57 Two—Sir Matthew Hale, and Simon, Lord Harcourt, by J. Simon

58 Two—Eliz. Duchess of Hamilton, by Finlayson, 1770, and Louise Henrietta de Hartefeldt, by V. Green

59 Five—Handel, William Hayes, by Thomas Park; Hevelius, James Hodgson, by G. White; and James Hutton, by J. R. Smith

60 One—Admiral Sir Charles Hardy, after Romney, by Dickenson—*fine*

61 Three—Sir Harry Harper, by J. R. Smith—*private plate*; Mr. Heath, town clerk of Exeter—*proof*; and Thomas How, Lord Mayor of Dublin, 1733, by J. Brooke

62 One—John Harrison, time-keeper, by P. Tassaert—*proof*—RARE, NOT IN BROMLEY

63 Three—Dr. John Hadly, 1759, by E. Fisher; Edmund Halley, and Sir Edw. Hulse, M. D. æt. 75, by J. Watson—*scarce*

64 One—Jonas Hanway, whole length, by Dunkerton—PROOF, FINE

65 Four—Simon, Earl Harcourt, by M'Ardel; Simon Harcourt, lord keeper, by Simon; William, Earl of Harrington, 1750, by Ford; and John, Lord Harvey, 1741, by Faber

66 Four—Simon, Earl Harcourt, by Fisher; William, Lord Harrington, by Simon; ditto, by Ford; and Robert, Lord Henley, by M'Ardel

67 Four—Benjamin Hallet, 1748, by James M'Ardel; Handel, John Harper, by Miller, 1739; first impression; and Mrs. Hartley, by W. Dickenson

68 One—Busick Harwood, M. D. by J. Jones

69 Two—Sir Walter Hawksworth, by G. Lumley; and Sir Isaac Herd—*private plates*—RARE

70 One—GEORGE HERIOT, JEWELLER TO KING JAMES VI.—Esplins—RARE

71 One—Sir Philip Honeywood, 1751, on horseback, by M'Ardel—SCARCE

72 Three—Mrs. Mariamne Herbert, by Faithorne; Lady Eliz. Harvey, by Simon; and John Harvey, Esq. by Tompson

73 One—Admiral Lord Hood, after Abbott, whole length, by V. Green—*fine*

74 Five—two, of Handeside; Edward Heardson, by J. R. Smith; James Hustler, &c.

75 One—Admiral Richard, Earl Howe, by T. Burke—*proof*

76 Two—CONSTANTIUS HUGENIUS, and CHRISTIANUS HUGENIUS, by A. Bloteling—FINE and RARE

77 One—Lady Amelia Hume, by Val. Green—*proof*

78 One—Osias Humphry, by ditto, ditto

CLERGY.

79 Three—Bishops—Thomas Herring, by M'Ardel; John Hoadley, 1733, by Faber; and George Hooper, of Bath, &c. by G. White

80 Two—Bishops—Thomas Herring, by M'Ardel; and John Hinchliff, of Peterborough, by John Young—*a proof*

81 Two—Bishops—John Hough, æt. 91, by Faber, and Henry Hubbard, by C. H. Hodges

82 One—Cardinal Howard, after Du Chatel, by J. Vander Bruggen—*rare*

83 Five—Thomas Hall, V. D. M. æt. 75, 1762, by Bockman; Aaron Hart, Rabbi, æt. 81, by M'Ardel, 1751; James Hervey, by Faber, 1751; Joseph Hussey, by ditto, 1722; and David Jennings, by M'Ardel

BY HOGARTH.

84 One—portrait of William Hogarth sitting painting, 1764

85 One—ditto, in the oval, 1749—*scarce*

86 Four—the bruiser, with the plain pallet; John Wilkes, Sir Robert Fagg, and Lord Lovet

87 One—Lady Frances Byron, whole length, by Faber, 1736—*very fine and scarce*

88 One—ditto, *ditto*

89 Two—Mr. Pine, with a stick; and one in an oval, by M'Ardel—*proof*

90 Two—Capt. Thomas Corans, 1739, and Daniel Lock, by M'Ardel—*fine*

91 One—SARAH MALCOLM, EXECUTED 1732—THE ORIGINAL VERY RARE

92 One—JAMES GIBBS, IN AN OVAL, by M'Ardel—FINE AND RARE

93 Six—the raree ſhow, Elizabeth Adams, &c.

94 Five—Gin. Lane, Beggar's Opera, Shrimps, &c.

95 Three—Satan, Sin, and Death, by Ogborne, &c.

96 One—Enthuſiaſm delineated

97 Twelve—publiſhed by Liveſay

98 One—ÆNEAS IN A STORM—RARE

99 Two—the analyſis of beauty, firſt ſtate

100 One—the Indian emperor, by Robert Dodd

101 One—the Beggar's Opera, by Blake—*proof*

102 One—the election, 1755, the ſecond ſtate, with the four hats—SCARCE

Eighth Day's Sale.

ENGLISH ENGRAVED PORTRAITS.

H

1 THREE—W. Van Haren, by A. Bloteling, 1680; D. Heinſus, and Lud. Holberg

2 Eight—Mary Howard, by Miller; Thanes autograph, &c.

3 Seven—Hampden, by Audran; Lord Hopton, Scrope Howe, &c.

4 Four—Charles, Earl of Halifax, by Drevet; Sir Henry Hobart, by S. Paſs, &c.

5 Three—Charles, Earl of Halifax, by Drevet; George, Marquis of ditto, by Houbraken; and Sir John Holt, by R. White

6 Seven—Aaron Hill, by Hulſbergh; Sir Robert Howard, by R. White; J. Hughes, by V. Gucht, &c.

7 Seven—Mrs. Hartley, by J. K. Sherwin; Miſs Harrop, by Delatré, &c.

8 Two—John Hall, by Marſhall; and Philemon Holland, by ditto

9 Four—James, Duke of Hamilton, by M. Drouſhout, 1623; ditto, 1648, by R. White; William, ditto, 1652, by ditto; and one by M. V. Gucht

10 One—James, Marquis of Hamilton, by Marſhall, quarto

11 One—COUNT HARCOURT, by MASSON—VERY FINE

12 Three—John Heywood, whole length, wood cut; and Richard Head—*ſcarce*

13 Two—Count Harcourt, by J. Morin; and George, Marquis of Huntley, by Voerſt—*ſcarce*

14 One—Philip, Lord Hardwicke, by B. Baron—*fine*

15 One—Sir JOHN HARRINGTON, with the watch, four Engliſh verſes, octavo—VERY RARE, not in Granger

16 Two—Buſick Harwood, M. D. by W. A. Gardiner, 1790; and Joſeph Haydn, by Schiavonetti, 1792

17 One—FRANCIS HAWKINS, æt. 10, by J. Payne—VERY FINE AND RARE

18 Five—Francis Hawkins, Benjamin Hewling, &c.

WENCESLAUS HOLLAR.

VARIOUS.

19 Five—from Aſhmole's order of the garter, &c.

20 A parcel of ditto, great ſeals of England, &c.

21 Twenty-ſeven—Habits—ORNATUS MULIEBRIS ANGLICANUS, 1640

22 One—the winter habit of an Engliſh gentlewoman, 1644—*very fine*

23 One—the Euchariſtical cup, after Andrea Mantegna, the original, 1640—FINE AND RARE

24 Fourteen—views of Tangier, 1673

25 Four—the combat between John de Aſtley and Sir Ph. Boyle in Smithfield, 1441; view of Hull, ditto of Richmond; and a map of England covered with armies, from Ruſhworth

26 Seven—ſmall views of Dover Caſtle, Elizabeth Caſtle, &c. &c.

27 One—the ſea-fight between the Engliſh fleet, under Prince Rupert and the Duke of Albemarle, and the Dutch fleet, under De Ruyter, 25th July 1666, with a liſt of the Engliſh ſhips, the number of their men and guns—VERY RARE

28 Two—THE TRIAL AND EXECUTION OF THOMAS, EARL OF STRAFFORD—VERY FINE

PORTRAITS.

29 Six—the American, the Turk, &c.

30 One—lady in an oval, fan in her left hand, 1652—*ſcarce*

31 One—Anne of Cleves, folio—*ſcarce*

32 One—ELIAS ALLEN, 1653—RARE AND FINE

33 One—Thomas, Earl of Arundel, in an oval, 1639—*fine*

34 One—the mauſoleum of the Earl of Arundel, who is ſitting on the tomb, various emblems of Death, Time, &c.—VERY RARE

35 One—ditto, a proof—EXTRA RARE

36 Three—Thomas, Earl of Arundel, in a ſquare, after Vandyck; Alathea, Counteſs of ditto, 1646; and Ann Bullen, a circle, 1649

37 Three—Alathea Talbot, L. Andrews, and Richard Bernard, æt. 74, 1641—*fine*

38 Three—Aretino, Daniel Barbaro, and Hus van der Borcht

39 One—J. Banfi Hunniades—very fine and rare

40 Three—Baſtwick, Laighton, and Prynne, with an hiſtorical account at the bottom of each

41 One—Francis Battallia, the stone-eater, with his hiſtory—very rare

42 Two—Richard Bernard, æt. 74; and William, Lord Brouncher, from Sprat, hiſtory of the Royal Society, 1667

43 One—the Daughter of George Villiers, Duke of Buckingham, in an oval, 1648

44 Two—One ditto, and Chriſtina, Queen of Sweeden, 1650

45 One—Edward Calver, of Wilbie, in the county of Suffolk—rare

46 One—Dr. Chambers, æt. 88, after Holbein, 1648

47 One—King Charles I. in an oval of palms, on a sheet, representing the several forms, how his army enquartered in the fields, in the march to Scotland, in 1639—very rare

48 Two—ditto, (with large roſes in his ſhoes) and his Queen, preſenting their crown and ſceptre to Mary of Medicis; and Charles II. when young, after Vandyck, ſmall folio

49 One—the Statue of Charles I. at Charing-Croſs

50 Two—Charles, Prince of Wales, Duke of Cornwall, 1630, in an oval, 1641; and Charles II. after Van Hoeck, octavo—*ſcarce*

51 One—Charles II. whole length, ſtanding on a pedeſtal, with emblems, after Cornelius Schult, 1650, ſheet—*fine*

52 One—Charles II. Sun rising in the back ground, after Diepenbeck, sheet—*fine*

53 Five—the Cavalcade of his Majesties passing through the City of London, towards his Coronation, 1661—*fine*

54 One—John Clenche, 1664, ditto

55 One—Sir Thomas Cromwell, 1546, ditto

56 One—ditto

57 One—Oliver Cromwell on horseback—*rare*

58 One—RICHARD CROMWELL, Lord Protector, &c. in a square

Note at the bottom of the Print by Mr. Hillier. "This portrait was etched by W. Hollar, "but he was afraid to put his name; and the Plate was destroyed as soon as Richard "resigned his pretensions to the Protectorship." VERY RARE.

59 Three—small ovals — Lord Cottington, Sir George Crooke, and Sir Edward Dering

60 Two—Lord Denny, in a circle, æt. 29, 1541, FINE; and John Diodati

61 One—LORD DIGBY, IN ARMOUR, after Vander Borcht—EXTRA RARE AND FINE

62 One—Edward VI. with the rattle, 1650—*rare*

63 One—Princess Elizabeth, daughter of King Charles I. in an oval, 1650—*rare*

64 One—Robert Devereux, Earl of Essex, standing, whole length, army in the distance, 1644—*fine and rare*

65 One—Robert Devereux, Earl of Essex, on horseback; under the horse a map of England, 1643—*first state of the plate, extra fine and rare*

66 One—William Fenner, under an arch, 1656, small folio

67 One—ditto, in a square, æt. 40, 1640—*rare*

68 One—Lady Gerald, anonymous, with an orange tree, in a ſquare, 1652—*rare*

69 Two—Sir Henry Guldeforde and Lady, in circles—*fine*

70 Three—Sir Harry Guldeforde; Hans Holbein, æt. 45, 1543; and the tomb of Archbiſhop Hacket, 1674

71 One—James Harrington, Eſq. in an oval, after P. Lely, 1658—*rare*

72 One—Robert Heath, 1664

73 Two—W. Hollar's own portrait, in an oval, æt. 40, 1647—ONE WITH VARIATIONS IN THE ARMS—EXTRA RARE

74 Four—ovals—Prynne; Henry, Earl of Huntingdon; Martin Tromp; and Mildmay, Earl of Weſtmorland

75 Three—Henrietta Maria, in a ſquare, 1641; John IV. King of Portugal, &c.

76 One—Killigrew, ſitting, leaning on a table, a quartered cap, and gown lined with female heads, ſquare

*76 One—a copy of ditto, larger, with variations—*rare and curious*

77 Two—Arthur Lake; and Hugh Lupus, Earl of Cheſter, ſitting in his parliament

78 Four—Elizabeth, Ducheſs of Lenox, after Vandyck; John Malder, after ditto, 1645; Mary de Medicis, in a ſquare; and Mr. Morett

79 One—Sir Samuel Moreland, in an oval—*rare*

80 Five—Maximilian, king of the Romans, at dinner; Moretite, &c.

81 One—Blaſii de Manfré, the water-ſpouter, in an oval, ſixteen latin lines—*fine and ſcarce*

82 Three—ditto; Nathaniel Nye and James Nailor, in the pillory and at the cart's tail

83 One—Nathaniel Nye—*fine*

84 One—Francis de Neuille, 1644—*fine*

85 One—William, Prince of Orange, on horſeback; married May 23, ſold by Thos. Jenner—*rare*

86 Three—William Oughtred, æt. 73, 1646; Charles, Count Palatine, after Vandyck, 1646; and Philip IV. of Spain, 1652

87 One—Philip, Earl of Pembroke, in an oval, after Vandyck—*fine*

88 Four—Jerom, Earl Portland, after ditto, in a ſquare, 1645; Maria, Counteſs Portland, 1650; Philip IV. of Spain, 1652; and Anne Maria, 1652

89 Two—Joannes de Reede, æt. 52, 1645, in an oval; and John Rogers, left hand on a table, ink-ſtand, ſix Engliſh verſes, 1653

90 Two—Richard II. at his devotion, kneeling by his three patron ſaints, &c. ſixteen latin verſes—*ſcarce*

91 One—Peter Paul Rubens, in a hat, &c. in an ornamented oval, on which hang two pallets with bruſhes—*very fine*

92 Three—Prince Rupert, in an oval, 1643; Duke of Suffolk, &c.

93 One—Thomas, Earl of Strafford, in armour, half length, after Vandyck, 1640—*fine*

94 One—ditto, *ditto*

95 One—Peter Smart, æt. 73, 1641—*fine*

96 One—Henry Howard, Earl of Surry, æt. 25, after Holbein, folio—*rare*

97 Three—Robert Sanderſon, 1658; Jane Seymour, in a circle, 1648; and Ralph Venning, æt. 37, 1673, in an oval

98 One—Major Wildman, in an oval of palm; view of St. Paul's, &c. 1653, inſcribed "*Nil admirari.*"—RARE

99 One—Hans Van Zurch, 1532, after Hans Holbein, 1647—*fine*

100 Two—ditto; and Lucas and Cornelius de Wael, after Vandyck, 1646

Ninth Day's Sale.

ENGLISH ENGRAVED PORTRAITS

CONTINUED.

H

1 ONE—Dr. Hayes, in an oval, grapes and roſes, by J. K. Sherwin, *private plate—rare*

2 One—Lord Heathfield, by Martin—*proof*

3 Four—Henrietta Maria, &c.

4 One—Henry, Prince of Wales, by C. Boel

5 Eight—Kings, Henry I. to the VIII. by Sherwin, Hall, &c.—*fine*

6 Eleven—Kings, by Eliſtrack, &c.

7 One—Henry III. of France, by Werix, 1647, folio—*fine*

8 One—Henry IV. of ditto, on horſeback, army engaging, trophies, &c. by Wolf. Kilian—*ſcarce*

9 One—ditto, by Fournier, with diamond buttons—*very rare and curious*

10 One—ditto, on horſeback, dogs, &c. hunting in the back ground, by ditto, 1600—*very curious*

11 One—ditto, by H. Goltzius—*fine and ſcarce*

12 —Six—Various, Henry III. and IV. of Frauce

13 One—Henry IV. by H. Hondius, 1630—*fine*

14 Two—Henry II. of France, 1547; and Henry IV. on horſeback, by A. Tempeſta, 1593

15 One—Henry VI. from the painting in King's College Chapel, by J. Bretherton, before the plate was reduced

16 Thirteen—Henry VIII. Catharine Howard, &c.

17 Two—Henry VIII. on his throne, with portraits of thirty kings and nobility, in proceſſion, by J. Sympſon —*printed on vellum and illuminated*

18 One—HENRY, PRINCE OF WALES, IN CLOAK AND TRUNK BREECHES, ſold by John Sudb and George Humble, folic—*very rare and curious*

19 Two—Daniel Heinſius, by Suyderhoef; and Conſt. Hugenius, by Lucas Vorterman—*fine*

20 Three—William Harvey, by Phil Phillipe; John Heydon, by T. Croſs; ditto, by W. Sherwin; and William Hervey, by Hall

21 Two—Nathaniel Highmore, by A. Bloteling, &c.

22 Four—Hobbs and Hampden

23 One—James Hodder, in an oval of foilage, by Gaywood—*ſcarce*

24 Two—ditto, in a ſquare, ſix lines; and William Hunt, by R. White

25 One—WILLIAM HODSON, by W. Marſhall—FINE AND VERY RARE

26 One—HENRY, EARL OF HOLLAND, Baron of Kenſington, four French verſes, by Cornelius Galle—FINE AND RARE

27 One—SIR JOHN HOTHAM, whole length — VERY RARE

28 One—Geneological Tree of the Howard family, with portraits of Queen Katharine Howard, Lady Agnes, Marchioneſs of Wincheſter, Mary Ducheſs of Somerſet, and Frances Ducheſs of Richmond, with armorial bearings—EXTREMELY RARE AND CURIOUS

29 Five—on India paper, by Houbraken; Anne of Denmark, Abbot, Sir Edward Coke, William Harvey, and R. Earl of Lindſey

30 Six—*proofs*, by ditto; Earl of Northumberland; Sir Edward Coke; Ireton; Duke of Lauderdale; Pym; and Sir William Temple

31 Seven—by ditto, William, Earl of Bedford; George, Duke of Buckingham; Oliver Cromwell; Lord Fairfax; R. Earl of Leiceſter; William, Lord Ruſſell; and Lord Torrington

32 Eight—by ditto, Earl of Arundel, Addiſon, Buchan, Sir F. Bacon, Sir N. Bacon, Chaucer, Dryden, and Sir William Temple

33 Eight—ditto, Earl of Arlington; George, Duke of Buckingham; Lord Burleigh; Sir F. Drake; Biſhop Fiſher; Sir Edward Coke; Lord Coventry; and Mary, Queen of Scots

34 Eighteen—Portraits to illuſtrate Granger, &c.

HISTORICAL, &c.

35 Twelve—various

36 Three—the new ſettlement at Sierra Leona, in colours

37 One—the inſide of St. Paul's, with their Majeſty's, &c. on his Recovery, 1789, by R. Pollard—*proof*

38 Three—Convalescence de Louis XIV. &c.

39 One—Death of Chatterton, after Singleton, by Orme

40 Ten—History of King Charles I.

41 One—Charles II. after his defeat by Cromwell, at the Battle of Worcester, after Stothard, by C. Knight—*proof*

42 Three—the Entertainment at the Hague, of Charles II. his Queen, &c. by Matham, Phillipi, &c.—*fine*

43 One—Henry IV. King of France, touching for the evil, P. Firens excudit

44 Eight—Charles VII. la Pucelle D'Orleans, &c. 1429, by J. Pouissart; Execution of Thomas, Earl of Strafford; Thomas Armstrong, &c.—CURIOUS

45 Two—the Death of Frederick Henry, Prince of Orange, 1647, by C. Van Daen, &c.—*scarce*

46 One—Marriage of the Pretender, 1789, by A. Friz—*scarce*

47 One—the Pope's doleful Lamentations for the unfortunate miscarriage of his several late plots, in ten compartments; the assassinating of Justice Arnold, Capt. Tom committed to Newgate, the Devil at breakfast, Faithorne? with letter-press description—*very rare and curious*

49 One—Coronation of the King of Bohemia, 1619—*ditto*

50 One—"A history of the new plot; or, a prospect of conspirators; their designs damnable, ends miserable, deaths exemplary;" in seven compartments; E. Shaftsbury dictating; ditto at Consult; Arthur, Earl of Essex, cut his own throat; Lord William Russell's execution in Lincoln's-Inn Fields, &c. with description, 1683—*ditto.*

51 One—England—memorial of its wonderful deliverance from the French tyranny and Popish oppression, performed through Almighty God's infinite goodness and mercy; his Highness William Henry of Nassau, the High and Mighty Prince of Orange, 1688—*ditto*

52 One—the treaty of Breda, July 31, 1667, with nine historical representations

53 Sixteen—relating to Charles II. King of Spain, &c. by P. Schenk

54 Eighty-two— ——— to James II. and William III. by Schoenebeck, &c.

55 Thirteen—ditto, by J. V. Vianen, 1690

56 Four—Coronation of William and Mary at Westminster, by Stoopendael; the reception of the King in London, &c.

57 Six—James II. in parliament, by J. Gole; visit of Henrietta Maria, and Prince William of Nassau, to Andrian Paw, 1644, &c.

58 Seven—Siege of Groeningen, &c.

59 Three—the young Pretender; Father Peters, &c.

60 Eleven—landing of William the Third; Mary, &c.

61 Three—Coronation of William and Mary, with the procession, &c.

62 Three—the departure of William VIII. ditto, on his throne in the parliament house, by R. de Hooge, &c.

63 Three—the coronation, by R. de Hooge, &c.

64 Eight—various, relating to William III.

65 Four—the departure and landing of William and Mary; the fleet, &c. by R. de Hooge

66 One—the flight of James II. and the battle of the Boyne, 1690

67 Four—the treaty at Breda, by R. de Hooge, &c.

68 Three—the reception of Mary, Princeſs of Orange; proceſſion of the coronation, with a view of Weſtminſter Hall; and the death of Mary, by R. de Hooge

69 Four—birth of the Pretender, &c.—*curious*

70 Four—various

71 One—treaty of Munſter, 1648, by Suyderhoef—*fine*

72 One—ditto, *ditto*

73 One—the four burgo-maſters, by Suyderhoef—*fine*

74 One—ditto

75 One—the inſtallation of the Earl of Weſtmorland in the theatre at Oxford, by T. Worlidge, 1761

76 One—the proſpect of the royal army, as encamped on Hounſlow-heath, 1688, with the arms of the colonels —*large ſheet, very rare*

77 One—the powder plot, 1605, with Guy Faux under a canopy; Count Gondamor, Father Peters, the Pope, &c.; view of the armada, 1588; Tylbury Camp, &c. invented by Samuel Ward, preacher, of Ipſwich, twelve Engliſh verſes, 1621—*a ſheet, very rare and curious*

78 One—James I. and Charles I. with all the monarchs of Europe ſitting under two tents, with labels, &c. in Engliſh—*very fine and rare*

79 Two—Cromwell diſſolving the Parliament, and the landing of Charles II. at Dover, after Weſt, by Woollett, Sharp, and Hall—*fine*

80 One—the laſt judgement, after Michael Angelo, by M. Rota—*fine and rare*

81 One—Lord Howe's victory on the 1ſt of June 1794, after M. Browne, by D. Orme—*proof*

82 One—Henry VIII. granting the charter to the barber-ſurgeons, by Baron, the etching—*rare*

83 Twenty-four—life of Chrift, by J. Parocel, on India paper

84 Two—from Boydell's Shakfpeare—Titus Andronicus, by Thos. Kirk; and Troilus and Creffida, from Romney, by Legat

85 Two—from ditto — All's well that ends well, after Wheatley, by Facius; and Romeo and Juliet, after Miller, by ditto

86 Two—the bubblers' mirrour, or England's folly — *fcarce*

87 One—THE ROYAL ACADEMY AFTER ZOFFANY, BY EARLOM—A CAPITAL PROOF

ENGLISH ENGRAVED PORTRAITS.

I

88 Four—Charles Jarvis, by Vander Gucht; J. Ingenhoufz, by Cunego, 1769; George Juan, by Carmona; and the Princefs Ifabella Cartoryfcka, by G. Teftolini

89 Eight—Gil Jacchæus, J. Jegon, by Tyfon; William Jones, by Sherwin, &c. &c.

90 Eleven—Portraits to illuftrate Grainger, &c.

91 Three—Hilldebrad Jacob, *proof*, by Houbraken; Dr. Samuel Johnfon, ditto, by Heath; and one by Holloway, with Thomas Edwards, Efq. &c.

92 One—five ovals of James IV. of Scotland; Margaret, Daughter to Henry VII. Archibald, Earl of Angus; Henry VII. and Elizabeth of York; with their coats of arms, &c.—*very rare and curious*

93 Eleven—Scotch Kings, &c.

94 Four—James I. ſitting with crown and ſceptre, by Simon Paſſe; a ditto, in an oval, by Thomas de Leu, octavo; one of ditto, ſtanding, in a triangle, ſurround with nine ſmall portraits of the Palatine family, &c. *curious*

95 JAMES I. AND JANE, QUEEN OF SCOTLAND, 1424, IN TWO SMALL OVALS—VERY RARE AND CURIOUS

96 Four—James I. and II.

97 One—James I. hat and feather, left hand on his ſword, four verſes, ſold by Stent—*ſcarce*

98 Eight—Scotch Kings, by Gaywood, &c.—*fine impreſſions*

99 One—James I. crowned with laurel, ſceptre in his right hand, by Criſpin de Paſs, 1613—*very fine and rare*

100 One—JAMES I. AND HIS QUEEN, whole length, Latin verſes at the bottom, the original print which is copied by WIERIX—ditto

101 Two—James I. ſitting on his throne, and family, containing fifteen portraits, by William Paſs, a ſheet—*extra rare and fine*; one, the ſame plate, with the addition of ſeven portraits on the left ſide, "The royale progenie of Charles I. and three on the right ſide of the Palatine family—VERY CURIOUS

102 Four—James II. the Duke of Albemarle, &c.

*102 Henry Ireton, Parliament-general, on horſeback—*ſcarce*

103 One—George, Lord Jeffreys, 1686, by R. White—*fine and ſcarce*

104 Two—Iſabella, Infanta of Spain, after Rubens, by John Muller, 1615; one ditto, by Suyderhoef, with ornamental border—*fine*

105 One—SIR THOMAS ISHAM, of Lamport, by D. Loggan, 1676—VERY FINE AND RARE

106 Three—Hadrian Junius, folio, by C. J. Vischer; Francis Junius, eight Latin lines; ditto, by Gunst

CLERGY.

107 Five—James Janeway, in an oval, four verses; Stephen Jay; Mr. Jones, of Langan, by Fittler, &c.

108 Two—Arthur Jackson, by D. Loggan; and Henry Jessey, æt. 63—*scarce*

Tenth Day's Sale.

FOREIGNERS.

I

1 SEVEN—Isabella, after Titian, &c.

2 Five—Jollyvet, by S. Gribelin; Vin. Justianus Josephi, by C. Mellan, &c.

3 Six—Popes—Innocent XI. by D. L. 1683; one of ditto, by J. Gole; Innocent XII. by Thomassin, folio; ditto, by ditto, from a medallion; Innocent XIII. folio, by Jac. Freij, 1722

4 Two—Equestrian statue of Joseph, late King of Portugal, with A PORTRAIT OF THE MARQUIS DE POMBAL, by V. Green; THE ETCHING OF DITTO —VERY RARE

5 Five—Jean Jouvenet, by An. Trouvain; Luc. Jordani, by J. B. Catenaro, &c.

6 One—Jourdan, whole length, mez. by Coqueret

ENGLISH MEZZOTINTO PORTRAITS.

I

7 Three—Countefs Jarnac, by Humphry; Frances, Countefs of Jerfey, by Watfon; and Mifs Jones, by V. Green—*proof*

8 One—Sir Lioline Jenkins, by H. Quites—*rare*

9 One—Sir Thomas Jones, Judge of the King's Bench, by R. Tompfon—*fcarce*

10 One—Admiral Sir Jofeph Jordan, by ditto—*fcarce*

11 Seven—Inigo Jones, by V. Green; Eyles Jrwin, by Walker, &c.—*proof*

12 One—William Innes, whole length, one of the fociety of Gofferers, by Val. Green—*private plate*

JESUITS.

13 One—Paul Atkinfon, æt. 73, an etching, quarto—*fcarce*

14 Three—Arrowfmith, Hurft, and Cuthbert Mayn, executed 1579, A. B. *fecit*

15 Five—Bel, Bullaker, Colman, Heath, and Woodcoke——*very fine*

16 Two—Bullakar and Bel—*very fine*

17 Two—Edmund Campian and Henry Garnet, folio

18 Three—Bel, John Fenwick, by M. Bouche; and Thos Pickering, æt. 53, 1670, in a circle

19 Two—Richard Reynolds, a Brigattin Monk of Sion-houfe, 1535; and Edward Oldcorn, 1606, by Bouttats—*fcarce*

20 Five—Henry Heath, 1643; Philip Powel, 1646; Wright, Benedictus Anglus, by Picart

21 Six—by Wierix, Bolswert, &c.

FOREIGNERS.

K

22 One—ADMIRAL KORTENAER—*fine*

23 Four—le Kain, by St. AUBIN—*fine*; Melchior Klesel, by A. Sadeler; Jan Kuiper, by Houbraken; and Andre Van Kruyssen, by Matham

ENGLISH MEZZOTINTO PORTRAITS.

K

24 One—The HON. SIR ARTHUR KAYE, OF YORK, by J. Simon—VERY RARE AND FINE

25 Two—Admirals—Richard Kempenfelt, by Richard Earlom; and Keppel, by W. Dickenson—*proofs*

26 Four—Augustus Keppel, by Dickenson—*proof*; Peter, Lord King, 1725; Colonel Richard King; and Evelyn, Duke of Kingston, by Faber, 1733

27 Two—Miss Kettle, playing on the guitar, by V. Green—*proofs*

28 Three—Anne Killegrew, by A. Bloteling; Mrs. Knight, the famous singer, by J. Faber, 1749; and Lucy Loftus, by Browne

29 One—THOMAS KILLEGREW, with a sword, in an oval, by J. Vander Vaart

30 A ditto—SQUARE PROOF BEFORE THE PLATE WAS MADE OVAL—VERY RARE

31 One—ditto, in oval, by ditto

32 Two—Edward King, M. D. 1684, by R. Williams—*fine*; and Madam Anne Kirk, whole length, by Beckett

33 One—John Knight, of Gosfield, with his wife and fon, by Faber, 1736—*fcarce*

ENGLISH ENGRAVED PORTRAITS.

K

34 Three—Sir Godfrey Kneller, William Kippax, by N. Parr; and Edward King

35 Three—Lord Kames; Alexander, Earl of Kellie, by R. Blyth; and William Kenrick, by Worlidge

36 Two—the Kentifh petitioners, by R. White; and Capt. Robert Knox, by ditto, 1695

37 Four—Mrs. Kirk, and Lady Morton, by J. Gronevelt, &c.

38 Two—Jofiah Keeling, difcoverer of the rye houfe plot, 1683, by R. White—*fine and fcarce*; and the copy

39 One—Sarah, Countefs of Kinnoull—*proof*, by Caroline Watfon, 1798—*very highly finifhed*

40 One—DITTO—IN COLOURS

*40 One—Edmund King, M. D. by R. White—*fine*

41 One—CHARLES JOHN, LORD KONINGSMARKE, folio, by R. White, 1682—VERY FINE AND RARE

42 Five—Benjamin Keach, æt. 54, 1699, fix verfes; Thomas Kenn, by Vertue; J. Glen King; W. B. Kirwan, by Nugent; and Han Knollis, æt. 67

FOREIGN PORTRAITS.

L

43 Eight—Comes Lesno, by Falck; Buonavito Lorini; Henry, Duc de Longeville, by P. Pontius; Jus Lipsius, by de Jode, &c.

44 Eight—Leonardus Lessius, by Bolswert; Charles de Lomenie, by W. Vallet; G. de Laubespine, &c.

45 One—the family of Leopold, Grand Duke of Tuscany, and Emperor of Germany, 1785

46 Eight—Lowendal, by Larmessin; C. A. de Lorraine, by Daulle; Anne, Duchess de Longueville; Maria, Reine de France, &c.

47 Six—Lewis XIV. P. Simon, &c.

48 Six—Lewis XI. by Morin; Lewis XIV. by R. Nantueil; Queen of ditto, by Pitau; Lewis XV. by J. Daullé, ditto by Larmessin; and ten portaits of Lewis XIV. in different ages, finely engraved, on one sheet

49 Three—Lewis XIV. by P. Vandrebranc; one of ditto, a three quarter, by N. Pitau, in armour—*proof*, &c.

50 Seven—various, of Emperor Leopold

51 Two—Julius Paulus de Lionne, by EDELINCK—FINE; and Jean Baptiste Lully, by Roullet

52 Five—Leopold, by J. Brower; one ditto, by Paul Pontius, in armour, *fine*; ditto, by C. Galle; ditto, in armour, hat and feather; and Leopold II. by Durmer

53 One—Lewis XVI. in his robes, A MOST CAPITAL PROOF, BY BERVIC—VERY RARE

54 Fourteen—various nobility, whole lengths in the dresses of Lewis XIV.

ENGLISH MEZZOTINTO PORTRAITS.

L

55 Two—Mr. Gilbert Knowles, æt. 49, 1723, by Faber; and the Hon. George Lee, L.L.D. by Faber—*scarce*

56 One—MAJOR GENERAL LAMBERT, IN ARMOUR, IN AN OVAL, BY PLACE—EXTRA RARE AND FINE

57 Four—John, Duke of Lauderdale, by Becket; a ditto, with his Duchess, by Williams; Nicolas Lechmere, by Val. Green; and Sir John Lowther, by Browne

58 Three—J. F. Lampe, by M'Ardel; Anthony Leigh, by Smith; and Richard Leveridge, by Vanden Myn, 1753

59 Two—Humphry, Viscount Lanesborough, whole length, by J. Brooks; and James, Lord Lifford, by Dickinson

60 Three—Largiliere, the painter, and family; R. Lovett, of Worcester, by R. Hancock; and Roger Long, 1769, by Fisher

61 One—Henry Laurens, sitting in a chair, whole length, by V. Green—*proof, fine*

62 Two—Nat. Lee, the poet, by J. Watts; and Richard Leveridge, by Pether—*proof*

63 One—Thomas, Earl of Leicefter, whole length, by Val. Green—*proof*

64 Two—William Lingen, Efq. by J. Brooks; and William, Duke of Leinfter, by C. H. Hodges

65 Three—the Hon. Bilfon Legge, by Houfton; Sir John Ligonier, by Brooks; and Gideon Erneft Loudon, by Pickler, 1788

66 Three—Mrs. Lemaiftre, by V. Green—*proof*; Kath. Countefs of Lincoln, by Purcell; and Princefs Louifa Anne, by Houfton

67 Two—Lucy Loftus, by Browne; and the Hon. Lady Lorne, by ditto—*fcarce*

68 Three—Marmaduke, Lord Longdale; John, Earl of Loudon, by Spooner; and the whole length, by Faber, 1755—*fcarce*

69 One—Sir Robert Ladbroke, ditto, 1748

CLERGY.

70 Two—Bifhop Edmund Law, of Carlifle, by W. Dickinfon, 1777; and Charles Lyttleton, ditto, 1770, by James Watfon

ENGLISH ENGRAVED PORTRAITS.

L

71 Eight—Alexander, Earl of Leven; Robert, Earl of Lindfey; Lenthal, by Paul, &c.

72 Seven—Leeuwenhoek, by De Blois; Ant. de Lomenie, by Lafne, 1637; Orlando de Laffus, &c.

73 Ten—Portraits to Granger, &c.

74 Five—N. L'Anier, by L. Vorſterman; Lithgow; Judge Lyttleton; Sir Edward Lyttleton, ſmall oval, *fine*; and Locke, by Vanderbank

75 Eleven—Lilly, Lyttleton, Leybourn, &c.

76 Three—Lamotraye, by La Cave; Levinz, by R. White; and George St. Lo, by Joſeph Nutting

77 Six—Lady Leambert, by W. Nutter, 1792; William Legge, by Orde; Maria Linley, by Ryder, &c.

78 Five—Labutte, by Baldrey; Jer. de la Lande; Jean Law, by Schmidt; Comte Lally, and Linnæus

79 Two—Dr. John Lambe, original and copy—*rare*

80 Four—General Leſley, ſeven Engliſh lines; one in armour, from Ricraft; Robert, Earl of Leiceſter, wood-cut, 1563, &c.—*rare*

81 Five—Thomas, Duke of Leeds, by R. White; L'Eſtrange, by ditto; and Leybourn

82 Two—Thomas, Duke of Leeds, by R. White; and Largilliere, by F. Chereau, 1715

83 Five—various, of Robert, Earl of Leiceſter

84 One—the Hon. Charles Leigh, of Leighton, by B. Baron SCARCE

85 Two—Edward Leigh, by John Chantry; and one ditto, by T. Croſs, ſquare—*ſcarce*

86 One—James, Duke of Lenox, by R. Vaughan—*fine and ſcarce*

87 One—ditto, by Voerſt, *ditto*

88 One—LOD. DUKE OF LENOX, &c. by Simon Paſſe—VERY RARE AND FINE

89 One—Sir Richard Levett, 1700, by R. White—FINE

90 Four—Lewis XIII. folio, by Henry Hondius, 1627; ditto, by Morin; Lewis XIV. by Vanſchuppen, 1660, &c.

91 One—Sir John Ligonier, on horseback, by P. Tangé, 1747—*scarce*

92 One—Robert, Earl of Lindsey, by Voerst—*fine and scarce*

93 Two—Samson Lennard, by R. Vaughan, &c.

94 One—Sir Martin Lister

95 One—Edward, Lord Lyttleton, by FAITHORNE

96 One—Robert, Earl of Leicester; Viscount Lisle, by Simon Passe—*fine and rare*

97 One—the Lord Justices of England, by R. White, 1695—*fine and scarce*

98 One—ditto, by La Fueille

99 One—LADY LYCHFELDE, by Vanderbanc — FINE RARE

CLERGY.

100 Four—A. Lake, Bishop of Bath, æt. 59, by J. Payne; Bishop Laud, by R. White; Robert Leighton, Abp. of Glasgow, by R. Strange, &c.

101 One—Thomas Lamplugh, Abp. of York, æt. 74, by P. Vandrebanc—this plate was afterwards altered

102 One—Bishop Laud, by D. Loggan—*very fine*

103 Seven—Charles Leslie, by F. Chereau; Edward Lake, by Vand. Gucht; Luther, by Preisler; and Richard Lloyd, &c.

104 Two—John Lightfoot, by R. White; and Christopher Love, in the pulpit, eight Dutch verses—*fine and scarce*

105 Five—Ignatius Loyala, by Wierix, in a square; a ditto, in a circle, by ditto; Dr. Lupton, 1637, &c.

106 Two—Ignatius Loyala, in an oval, surrounded with twenty-nine ovals, historical of his life, by Francis Villamena—*curious*; and M. Luther, by W. Trevethen

107 One—ditto, in a large oval, by C. Vermeulen

108 Two—ditto, kneeling, by F. Poilly, folio; one an unfinished proof

109 One—Bishop William Lloyd, by D. Loggân—*fine and scarce*

Eleventh Day's Sale.

FOREIGN PORTRAITS.

M

1 NINE—Maximilian, Duke of Burgundie, by Suyderhoef; Pierre Maugis, by Morrin, &c.

2 Seven—Jule Manſart, by Simonneau; Johannes A. Marck, by A. V. Zylvelt; Thomas Maurois, by A. Conradus; Johannes Muller, by Falck; Bar. Morillus, by Richard Collin; Jo. An. de Maroulle, by Thomaſſin; and F. Malier

3 Four—Marie Thereſe, by N. de Poilly; ditto, by G. Edelinck; François de Maintenon, by Giffart; Diane de Monteſpan, by J. Gole

4 Seven—Franciſcus de Moura; Claude de Marolles, by Mellan; Michael de Marolles, by ditto; François, Duc de Modene, by Froſne, &c.

5 Four—Cardinals—Mazarine, by Jean Valdor; a ditto, by Mellan; a ditto, by Morin; a ditto, by Laſne

6 Three—Zacherias de Mez; Mazarine, by Nantuil, 1656; and F. Muguet, by Thomaſſin

7 Twelve—Machiavel; Marinus; Magliabechi; Maleſherbe, by L. Vorſterman, &c.

8 One—Duke of Maine, BY DREVET—*proof before the arms were eraſed*

9 Six—Marie, Reine de France, in her robes, by Larmeſſin; a ditto, in an oval, by ditto; Marie Thereſe, quarto, &c.

10 Six—Mignard, by Vermeulen; Vander Meulin, by Van Schuppen; Carlo Maratti, by Jac. Freij; Manſart, &c.

11 Two—Moreau and Maſſena, whole length, mez. by Coqueret

12 One—KARA MUSTAPHA BASSA, mez. by Becket—*rare*

13 Five—a ditto, by J. Gole; Francis Moroſini, by R. White, &c.

ENGLISH MEZZOTINTO PORTRAITS.

M

14 Three—Dodington, Ducheſs of Mancheſter, by Faber; Sarah, Ducheſs of Marlborough, and Lady Molyneux, by V. Green—*proof*

15 Three—Charles, Duke of Marlborough, by W. James; Admiral Matthews, by G. Johanſon, 1744; and Robert, Viſcount Moleſworth, by P. Pelham, 1721

N

16 One—George, Duke of Marlborough, whole length, in his robes, by John Jones—*fine*

17 Two—George, Lord Macartney, by Hudſon, *proof*; and John, Duke of Montagu, by J. M'Ardel—*ſcarce*

18 Three—Thomas, Earl of Macclesfield, by Simon; Anthony Malone, by Spooner; and James Mingay, by Hodges—*proof*

19 Two—Sir Herbert Mackworth, by Deane; and Dr. Moore, by Keating

20 Five—Queen Mary, by Faithorne, *proof*; Mary, of Eſte, by R. Williams, folio, *fine*; a ditto, by ditto, quarto; Mary, Queen of Scots, and Margaret, Queen of Henry VI. by Faber

21 One—Queen Mary, with a high head-dreſs—*ſcarce*

22 Two—John, Earl of Melfort, by Becket; and Lady Jane Middleton, J. Savage, *excud.*

23 Two—John, Earl of Melfort, and the Ducheſs of Mazzarino—John Lloyd, *excud.* a reverſe

24 One—Joe Millar, in the character of Teague, by A. Millar, 1739—*ſcarce*

25 One—John Milner, Eſq. whole length, by Faber—*very fine*

26 Two—James, Duke of Monmouth, by Schenck; and Ann, Ducheſs of Monmouth, by Vander Vaart—*fine*

27 One—James, Duke of Monmouth, on horſeback, by Capt. William Baillie, 1774

28 One—ditto, by Vander Vaart—*fine*

29 Two—Mary, Ducheſs of Montagu, by Faber, 1740; and Mudge, clock-maker, by Townly—*proofs*

30 One—Edward Wortley Montague, by J. R. Smith—*proof*

31 One—John Mortimer, by V. Green—*proof*

32 One—Charles, Baron Mountjoy, whole length, by V. Green

33 One—John Moyser, of Beverly, by Place—*very fine and rare*

34 Three—Thomas, Earl of Macclesfield; Arthur Manwaring, by Simon; and Alexander Murray, Esq. 1751, by Faber

35 Five—Sir William Musgrave, by J. R. Smith; Mr. Monox, of Suffolk; John Milton, by Faber, &c.

CLERGY.

36 Three—Samuel Madden, by John Brooks; ditto, æt. 68, 1755, by Richard Purcell; and Maxfield and family, by Dawe—*proof*

37 One—Lodowick Muggleton, æt. 90, 1697-8, in an oval—*rare*

38 Three—Samuel Madden, by Brooks; and Thomas Newton, Bishop of Bristol, by Earlom, 1767, &c.

39 One—John Moore, Bishop of Ely, 1691, by W. Faithorne—*fine*

ENGLISH ENGRAVED PORTRAITS.

M

40 Five—John Marten, by George White; Richard Mead, M. D. by Baron, 1749; Alexander Monro, M. D. by Basire, 1770; and Richard Morton, M.D. by Ad. Halweg; and Dr. Maddock, by Trotter

41 Four—Princess Mary, by Caroline Watson; Madam Mara, by Collyer; Mrs. Marshall, and Lord Moira, by Collyer

42 Four—Dr. Mead, by Baron; Mary Louisa, daughter of James II. by Parr; and Sarah, Duchess of Marlborough

43 Five—Mercier and family, an etching; Nicolas Mesnager, octavo; Peter Molinues; John Meerman, by Houbraken; and Montesquieu

44 Three—N. Mesnager, by Simonneau Major, 1715; Earl Marischal, an etching, profile; de la Mothe, by L. Spirinx, 1663; and John Meerman

45 Five—by Worlidge, Mahomet, a Turkish Merchant, Hamet, Admiral Mostyn, &c.—*two proofs*

46 Eight—various, Harding, &c.

47 Six—Portraits to illustrate Granger

48 Eighteen—Thane's Autographs, &c.

49 Eight—Massinger, by Grignon; John Milton, by Dolle, &c.

50 Six—Ever. Maynwaring, by R. White; Henry Maydman, V. Hove; Menasseh Benj. Israel, by Rembrandt; Milton, &c.

51 Five—Ever. Maynwaring, by R. White, with a plain band; Sir Henry Morgan, &c.

52 One—Captain Macbride, by James Fittler

53 One—RICHARD, LORD MAITLAND, 1683, by P. Vandrebanc—FINE AND SCARCE

54 One—Lord Mansfield, by D. Martin, 1775

55 Two—John, Earl of Marr, by P. Vandrebranc; and George, Earl of Melvill, by R. White—*fine old impression*

56 One—Patrick, Earl of Marchmont, 1698, by R. White, with armorial bearings, half sheet—*fine and rare*

57 Three—Gervase Markham, Robert May, and John Mayne, by M. Marlow—*fine and scarce*

58 One—John, Duke of Marlborough, in armour, half sheet

59 One—MARY, QUEEN OF SCOTS, in an oval, half sheet, vigniettes, at the corners of her execution, twenty Latin verses—*fine old impression*

60 One—ditto, superbly dressed, with a view of her execution, by J. Couway

61 Two—ditto, after J. Oliver, J. K. Sherwin, with ornaments—*proof, one on satin*

62 Eight—various, of Mary, Queen of Scots; and Mary of Medici, &c.

63 Four—ditto

64 One—Mary de Medicis, by Joan Wierix, 1600—*fine and rare*

65 One—Prince Maurice, on horseback, view of Nieuport, an army, &c. by Crispin de Passe, 1600

66 One—ditto, same plate, when young

67 One—EDWARD MASCALL, by JAMES GAMMON—FINE AND RARE

68 Two—Maximilian, the Emperor, &c. by Suyderhoef, with rich borders—*fine*

69 Two—Maximilian, by A. Durer

70 One—Maria de Medicis, by Sompel—*fine*

71 One—Duchess of Mazarin, by G. Valck

72 Two—H. Mill, from the night search, 1646—*very fine and rare*, and the copy

73 Two—John Milton, by Caroline Watson—*one a proof the head only*

74 One—James, Duke of Monmouth, on horſeback, ſold by S. Lye

75 One—ditto, in his robes, by A. Bloteling

76 One—ditto, ditto

77 Two—James, Duke of Monmouth; and Anne, Ducheſs of ditto, in ovals, ſupported by Cupids, quarto—*fine and very rare*

78 One—James, Duke of Monmouth, with the portraits of Armſtrong, Corniſh, &c. in eight ovals, ſold by J. Savage—*fine*

79 One—ditto, ditto

80 One—ditto, by P. Vandrebanc, a ſheet—*fine*

81 Five—Montroſs, quarto, one ditto, by Pontius, octavo; Sir John Meldrum, &c.

82 Five—Sir Thomas More, by Elſtrack, &c. Sir James Moore, by Yeates, &c.

83 One—Sir Thomas More and his family, the outline after Holbein, by Cochin—*very rare*

84 One—Robert Moriſon, M. D. of Aberdeen, 1683, by R. White, in an oval of flowers—*fine old impreſſion*

85 One—Philip, Earl of Mountgomery, by Voerſt, 1630—*very fine*

86 One—Sir Henry Mountague, by F. Delaram, ſix Latin verſes—*ſcarce*

87 One—Lieutenant-General Thomas Muſgrave, by G. S. Facius, 1797—*private plate*

CLERGY.

88 Ten—M. Malard; T. Manton, by R. White, folio; a ditto, octavo; Robert Markham, by Skelton, 1790, &c. &c.

89 Six—Manton, folio, by White; John March, B. D. by J. Sturt; Richard Meggot, by R. White; Henry More, by D. Loggan, folio; and Lod. Muggleton, by Cassel

90 One—TOBIAS MATTHEW, Archbishop of York, æt. 78, 1624, by R. ELSTRACK, eight Latin verses

91 One—PETER MEWS, Bishop of Winchester, by D. LOGGAN—*fine and rare*

92 Two—Richard Middleton, by R. Elstrack, 1617; and Samuel Moore, æt. 30, 1647, by W. Marshall, eight verses—*rare*

93 Three—Alexander More, by W. Passe, folio; John Moore, Bishop of Norwich, 1691, by R. White, &c.

94 Two—Alexander More, folio, in a square; a ditto, in a circle, by L. Visscher, ten French verses

FOREIGN PORTRAITS.

N

95 Five—Maurice, Count Nassau, by Matham; Lud. de Coligni, Countess Nassau, by Delff; and three others of the Nassau family

96 Three—William, of Naſſau, by Hondius, 1628; Wm Lewis, Count Naſſau, by And. Stock, 1614; and one ditto, by Delff, 1633

97 One—Admiral Van Nes—*fine*

98 Three—ditto; Henry, Count Naſſau, by P. V. Sompel; and Renatus Naſſau, by J. Suyderhoef

99 Two—Necker l'hommage ſincere, by Amicus; and David Nuyts, by J. Suyderhoef

100 One—John Maurice of Nassau, after G. Flinck, by C. V. Dalen—*very fine*

101 Six—John Nieuhoff; P. le Nevoux, by Poilly; John Neyen, by Muller, and three others

Twelfth Day's Sale.

ENGLISH MEZZOTINTO PORTRAITS.

N

1 THREE—Richard Naſh, by Bockman; William Neild, ſeven verſes, 1777, by J. Jenner; and Charles Newby, by Faber, 1744

2 Two—Cornelius Nary, C. F. P. Dr.; and Robert, Lord Newport, by Andrew Miller, 1747—*ſcarce*

3 Two—John, Baron Naas, by Charles Townley, 1777; and Lord Newport, by Miller—*ditto*

4 One—the Nabob of Arcot, by Dixon—PROOF

5 Two—Gray Nevil, 1720, by G. White—*one a proof*

6 Three—William, Lord Newbattle, by E. Fiſher, 1769; ditto, with Lady Elizabeth Keer, by V. Green; and George, Viſcount Newnham, by ditto—*both proofs*

O

7 Three—Thomas, Duke of Newcaſtle, in an oval, by Peter Pelham; ditto, in robes of the garter, by M'Ardell—*proof*; and Louis, Duc de Nivernois, by ditto

8 One—Abraham Newland, Eſq. by J. Grozer

9 One—Frederick, Lord North, by T. Burke—*proof*

10 Three—Madam Catherine Nevill, by Browne; George, Duke of Northumberland, in an oval, quarto, by Williams; and Elizabeth, Counteſs of Northumberland, by Beckett

11 One—GEORGE FITZROY, EARL OF NORTHUMBERLAND, after H. Gaſcar—*proof*, before the name of Tooker, exc. folio—VERY RARE

12 Two—Hugh, Duke of Northumberland, 1772, by Finlayſon; and Hugh, Earl Percy, the preſent Duke, by V. Green—*proofs*

13 One—Lady Elizabeth Newnham, by Val. Green—*proof*

CLERGY.

14 Five—Thomas Newcomb, by Faber, 1723; Samſon Occom, by Spilſbury; Robert Orme, M. A.—*ſcarce*; John Owen, by J. Vandevelde; and Titus Oates, by Tompſon

ENGLISH ENGRAVED PORTRAITS.

N

15 Nine—S. G. Noverre, by J. K. Sherwin, &c.

16 Four—Thomas Neale, by W. Marſhall; A. Noailles, &c.

17 Five—Sir Edward Nicholas, by Hertocks—*fine*: Sir Isaac Newton, by Hoare, &c.

18 Three—William, Duke of Newcastle, by Vorsterman; John, Duke of Newcastle, by R. White, &c.

19 Two—John, Duke of Newcastle, by R. White; and Heneage, Earl of Nottingham, 1681, by R. White

20 One—William, Duke of Newcastle, by Vorsterman —*fine*

21 One—Charles, Duke of Norfolk, whole length, after Gainsborough, by J. K. Sherwin, 1790—*private plate*

22 One—Thomas, Duke of Norfolk, with the staff of Earl Marshal, by ditto

23 One—HENRY, EARL OF NORTHUMBERLAND, 1619, by F. Delaram—RARE

24 One—Algernon, Earl of Northumberland, collar of the garter, &c.—*scarce*

25 One—CHARLES, EARL OF NOTTINGHAM, by PASSE—FINE AND RARE

26 Two—Heneage, Earl of Nottingham, 1681, by R. White; and Daniel, Earl of Nottingham, by Houbraken

27 One—CHARLES, EARL OF NOTTINGHAM, on horseback, view of the Armada, 1588, &c. folio—FINE AND EXTRA RARE

CLERGY.

N & O

28 Five—John Nelſon, æt. 66, by Harriſon, 1774; Rev. Mr. Newton, Benjamin Newton, by G. V. Gucht; Nicoll, by Worlidge; and Samuel Ogden

29 Five—Nalton, Chriſtopher Neſſe, æt. 56, 1678; William Nichols, by M. V. Gucht; William Outram, by R. White; and John Owen, by ditto

30 Six—Nicoll, by Worlidge; John Newte, by Vandergucht; William Nichols, by ditto; Ogden; James Owen, by Sutton; Nichols, &c.

31 Fifty-nine—Portraits from the Non-conformiſts Magazine

FOREIGN PORTRAITS.

O

32 Three—Philip, Duke of Orleans, oval, in armour, 1620; one ditto, on horſeback, by N. Bazin, 1686; and one ditto in oval

33 Five—Duke of Orleans, by Horthemels, 1716; Elizabeth, Ducheſs of ditto, by ditto; Anne Maria Louiſa D'Orleans, by C. Vermeulen, 1691; and two others of the Orleans family

34 Three—The Maid of Orleans, whole length; Count Octavio, by Vorſterman, &c.

35 Four—Cardinal Otthoboni, by J. Andran, &c.

36 One—Count Olivares, after Rubens, by P. Pontius

ENGLISH MEZZOTINTO PORTRAITS.

O

37 Four—Lady Susan O'Brien, by James Watson; Richard Oliver, 1772, by W. Dickenson; Miss Osborne, by ditto; and Thomas Otway

38 Five—William Henry, Prince of Orange, by Skenck, 1684; ditto, in a square, small, by A. Bloteling; Mary, Princess ditto, ditto, ditto, by Faithorne; and William Charles, Prince of Orange, 1734, by Faber

39 Two—William, Prince of Orange, and Mary, by Williams—*fine*

40 Two—ditto, by G. Valck

41 One—Frederick Henry, and Emelia, Prince and Princess of Orange, after Jordans, by Rymsdyk, 1767—*proof*

42 Four—William, Prince of Orange, by Faber, 1735; ditto, and Princess Ann, in one sheet, by ditto; Ann, Princess, by Simon, 1728; and Princess of Orange, by V. Green

43 Two—Edward, Earl of Oxford, 1715; and James, Duke of Ormond, by R. Williams, in ovals—*fine*

44 Two—General James Oglethorpe, by T. Burford; and Count Orloff, by Charles Townly, 1783

45 One—William, Lord Osborne, with his sisters Lady Bridgett and Lady Mary, by R. Williams—*scarce*

46 Two—Edward, Earl of Orford, in a small oval; and Robert, Earl of Oxford, by Smith, 1714

47 One—JOHN OVERTON, æt. 68, 1708—VERY RARE

ENGLISH ENGRAVED PORTRAITS.

O

48 Six—Thomas Ollyffe, the writing-mafter, &c.

49 Three—John Ogilby, by Lombart; a ditto, by W. Marfhall, 1649; and Thomas, Earl of Offory, 1680, by S. F. Ravenet

50 One—Titus Oates, infcribed "*Robert Ferguson, the raree-fhow; or Mamamouchee Mufty*," twenty-one Englifh verfes—*fine and rare*

51 One—Titus Oates, in the pillory; vignette of his being whipped; around the print are feven ovals of Jefuits, viz. Baker, Waring, Turner, Fenwick, Gavin, Harcourt, and Evans—*fcarce*

52 One—ditto, infcribed "*Teftis Ovat*," twenty-four Latin and Englifh verfes, fold by Hindmarfh, 1685 —*fine and very rare*

53 Five—Count Orloff, folio; Admiral Obdam, by B. Picart, 1728; Earl of Offory, by Ravenet, &c.

54 One—a Dutch Admiral, *proof*, by Arnold de Jode—if Obdam?

55 Two—William, and Mary Princefs of Orange, by Suyderhoef, 1643—*fine*

56 Two—William, Prince of Orange, by C. Viffcher, folio; and Philip, Prince of Orange, by Delff, 1628 —*fine*

57 Three—Mary, Princefs of Orange, by P. Bouttats; W. C. Hen. Prince of Orange, 1751, by Balchou; and one other, a *proof*

58 One—William II. Prince of Orange, whole length, by L. Laillier—*fine*

59 Five—Fred. Hen. Prince of Orange, by Van Meurs, &c. &c.

60 Two—W. C. Hen. Prince of Orange, by Balechou; and Fr. Henry, Prince of Orange, by Delff, 1633—*fine*

61 Twelve—Princes and Princeſſes of Orange, by Houbraken and Tanjé—*fine*

62 Two—William, Prince of Orange, æt. 23, 1649, by Cris Quebren; and the marriage of William, and Mary, daughter of Charles I. 1647

63 Four—William, Prince of Orange, quarto, by Henry Hondius, 1641, &c.

64 Four—William, Prince of Orange, on horſeback, with hat and feather, ſold by Stent; ditto, and Mary, Princeſs of Orange, whole length, &c.

65 Three—Hen. Fred. Prince of Orange, a three-quarter, by Delff; Prince Maurice, ſtanding, in armour, whole length, with army and fleet, by Sanredam, &c.

66 Four—William V. by P. Tanjé, 1755; and Anne, Princeſs of Orange, by Endlinck

67 One—William III. when Prince of Orange, on horſeback, hat and feather, the horſe's mane and tail reach the ground—*curious*

68 One—William, Prince of Orange, ſtanding, whole length, cap and feather, hand on a dog, a flower-pot, &c.—*ſcarce*

69 Two—William and Mary, by C. Viſſcher, 1649

70 One—William III. when Prince, leaning on a helmet, by P. Phillippe, half ſheet—*fine*

71 One—Maurice, Prince of Orange, hat and feather, left hand on his ſword, after A. V. Venne, by W. Delff—*fine*

72 One—the Princes of Orange on horſeback, by W. Delff, 1623, a ſheet—*fine and rare*

73 One—Henriette, Ducheſs of Orleans, large half ſheet —*fine and rare*

74 One—JAMES, DUKE OF ORMOND, folio, by D. Loggan—VERY FINE AND RARE

75 One—James, Duke of Ormond, on horſeback, 1713 —RARE

76 Three—Duke of Ormond, by S. F. Ravenet; ditto, by Gribelin; and the Earl of Orford, by Houbraken

77 One—THOMAS, EARL OF OSSORY, by P. Vandrebanc, large half ſheet—*fine and ſcarce*

78 Two—John Oxenſtirn, by P. de Jode, 1648; and Axel. Oxenſtirn, by Delff, 1636

P

79 Ten—George Parker, &c.

80 Five—Dr. Parſons, by Wilkin; Anthony Paſquin, by Wright, &c.

81 Six—Sir Walter Pringle, by Cooper; Colonel Parſons, by Gribelin; William Pattiſon, &c.

82 Three—Iſaac Pennington, in the Committee on Popery, in Maſquerade; Gal. Palmer, by R. White; and John Playford, by Van Hove

83 Ten—Gal. Palmer, by R. White; Samuel Pepys, by ditto, &c.

84 Sixteen—Thanes autographs, &c.

85 Six—Leonard Plukenett, 1690, by Collins; John Partridge, by R. White; Perkins, by Drapentier; Playford, by V. Hove, &c.

86 Five—Philip II. of Spain; Polyander, and Philaras, by Mellan

87 Five—Had. Paw, by Holftein; Patin, Nicol. Pirot, by Huret; and Polyander, by Delff

88 Four—Czar Peter, by Wagner; ditto, by P. Souberan; Jean Philips, by Endlinck; and Gen. Paoli, by Townley

89 Three—Charles Patin, by Le Fevre; ditto, by Maffon; and the Patin family, 1684

90 Two—Adrian Paw, ftanding, left arm on a book, half fheet; and Reg. Paw, æt. 67, by Theophilus Matham

91 One—William, Earl of Pembroke, by Voerft, 1633—FINE AND SCARCE

92 One—ditto, by Lucas Vorfterman—FINE and SCARCE

93 One—Philip, Earl of Pembroke, and family, after Vandyck, by B. Baron, 1740

94 One—James, Earl of Perth, 1682, after Kneller, by R. White, with armorial bearings

95 One—ditto, after Riley, by ditto, 1686, with ditto

96 One—Philip II. by Wierix, 1586, before the letters H. V. L. on the right-hand fide—*fine and rare*

97 One—ditto, by Viffcher—*fine*

98 Two—one ditto, by Baptifta Parmenfis, 1589, within a border of arms; and Philip the good

99 One—ditto, with a border of emblems, by Manellus Clodius, 1588—*rare*

100 One—John Philips, by M. Vander Gucht—*fine and fcarce*

101 One—Sir Thomas Pilkington, Lord Mayor, by R. White, 1691—*fine and rare*

102 One—the Right Hon. William Pitt, by J. K. Sherwin—*proof*

103 One—John Polyander, by Suyderhoef, 1641—VERY FINE

104 One—LOUISE, DUCHESS OF PORTSMOUTH, IN AN ELEGANT LACED DRESS, WITH HER SON AS A CUPID, after N. Gascar, by St. Baudet—VERY RARE AND FINE

105 One—Percival Pott, by R. M. Paye, 1783

106 Seven—antient printers, from Ames—*proofs, very scarce*

107 Six—the original drawings of ditto, by W. Faithorne, jun.—*very curious*

Thirteenth Day's Sale.

FOREIGN PORTRAITS.

P

1 EIGHT—Ben. Pictetus, by Houbraken, &c.
2 Ten—Father Paul; Alexander Polito, by Franceſchini; F. Pogge, by Picart, &c.
3 Ten—Popes—Paul IV. V. &c.
4 Three—Louis Picon, by Chereau; F. Pinſſon, by V. Schuppen; and Madam Peliſſier, by Daullé
5 Three—Philip IV. of Spain, and his Queen, after Rubens, by P. Pontius; and Philip V. by G. Vermeulen
6 Six—Kings of Spain
7 Four—with rich ornaments, by Suyderhoef, &c.
8 Seven—Cardinal Richelieu, by Nantuil; one of ditto, by Mellan; Cardinal Rochefocault, by Laſne, &c.
ur—N. Pouſſin, by J. Peſne; Palladio, by B. Picart; Peſne, by Trouvain, &c.

ENGLISH ENGRAVED PORTRAITS

CONTINUED.

CLERGY.

P

10 Six—Parnell, Peckwell, by Fittler; Samuel Pegge, by Basire; Christopher Pitt, &c.

11 Six—Edward Pearse, æt. 40, 1673, by R. White; John Pearson, æt. 70, by W. Elder; William Perkins, 1602, by R. Elstrache; Joseph Perkins, by R. White; John Preston, by W. Marshall, 1636; and Bishop Prideaux

12 Six—Pearson, by Elder; Nicolas Pearson, by Van Houe, four verses; John Piggot, by R. White; Samuel Pomfret, by Drapentier; John Preston, by Glover, nine verses; and a ditto, in a square twelves —*scarce*

13 Six—Parker, by Vertue, folio; Bishop Edward Parry, by J. Dickson—*rare*; John Pearson, by Elder; Bishop John Prideaux, &c.

14 One—Bishop John Pearson, by D. Loggan, *proof*, before the arms and name of engraver

15 Two—Vincent de Paul, by Boulanger; and Philip Neophytus, by R. White, 1702—*scarce*

16 One—WILLIAM PERKINS, IN AN OVAL, ON ONE SIDE, JESUS CHRIST, AND THE OTHER MOSES, &C. BY T. MATHAM—PROOF, VERY RARE AND FINE

17 Two—DAVID PRIMROSE, *rare*; and John Quick, æt. 55, by Sturt

18 One—SAMUEL PURCHAS, æt. 48, in the title complete, 1625

ENGLISH MEZZOTINTO PORTRAITS.

P

19 Four—Miſs Anne Parr, by Dean; Carey, Counteſs of Peterborough, whole length, by Faber; Conſtantia Philips, octavo, by ditto; and Lady Beauchamp Procter, by James Watſon

20 Two—Sir Hugh Palliſer, by J. R. Smith; and General Phillips, by V. Green

21 Two—Humphry Parſons, with the inſignia of Lord Mayor, and his coat of arms, four verſes, ſold by William Banks; and ditto, in an oval, with ditto, church and mitre, &c. in the corners, eight verſes—*ſcarce*

22 One—Admiral Sir Hyde Parker, by Charles Townley, 1785—*ſcarce*

23 One—ditto Sir Thomas Paiſley, 1794, by ditto

24 One—ditto, ditto

25 Five—Dorothy Packington, by V. Green; Mary, Counteſs Pembroke, 1443, by Faber; Queen Philippæ, by ditto; Villiers Clara Pitt, 1758, by M'Ardel; and Madam Plowden, by Faithorne

26 Three—Sir Richard Pearſon, by James Watſon—*proof*; Matthew Peters, by James Murphy; and William, Duke of Portland, by J. R. Smith

27 Two—Miſs Harriot Parrot, and Lady Pennyman, by V. Green—*proofs*

28 Two—the Right Hon. Henry Pelham, with John Roberts, Eſq. by Houſton; and William Pulteney, Eſq. by Simon

29 One—Pelham and his ſecretary—*proof*

30 Three—John, Lord Percival, by Faber, folio; Sir Philip Percival, by ditto, 1744, octavo; and Sir John Philipps, by ditto, 1748

31 Two—Thomas Penn, 1751, by Martin; and Silveſter Petyt, 1701, by G. White—*fine and ſcarce*

32 One—Pichegru, whole length, by Coqueret

33 Three—Sir John Philipps, by Faber; Pinchbeck, by ditto, in an oval; and Percival Pott, in an oval, after Dance

34 One—the Right Hon. William Pitt, by Richard Houſton, 1766, large

35 Four—Eight poets, Pope Prior, &c. by Kyte, in ovals

36 Two—Don Carlo, Earl of Plymouth, J. Lavaree, ex. and Louiſa, Ducheſs of Portſmouth, by G. Valch, 1678—VERY FINE

37 One—Powell, Benſley, and B. Smith, in King John, by V. Green—*proof*

38 One—Mr. Charles Poyſer, by Charles Townley—*proof*

39 Three—Alexander Pope, profile, laurel chaplet; Mat. Prior, by Faber, 1728; and Jean Jac Rouſſeau, by Corbett

CLERGY.

40 Two—Roger Pickering, by T. Burford, 1747; and Joseph Pullen, M. A. in an oval—*rare*

41 Three—Thomas Parnell, D. D. John Pelling, 1750, by M'Ardel; and Samuel Pomfret, æt. 71, 1721, large quarto

42 OLIVER PLUNKETT, 1681, by J. Vander Vaart—*fine and rare*

THE PALATINE FAMILY.

43 Five—Charles Lewis, Count Palatine, by de Jode, 1654; Charles Gustavus, by C. Galle, 1650; Ferdinand Maria, 1656, by de Jode; and Charles Theodore, Elector Palatine, by F. Verelst, 1771

44 Two—Charles Lewis, by Corn. Vischer, 1650; and Maximilian, after Sandrart, 1643, by M. Natalis

45 One—Prince Frederick Henry, 1630, sold by William Webb, quarto—*fine*

46 Four—Frederick V. folio, by L. Killian; and two by, Gunst—*proofs*

47 Two—Frederick, King of Bohemia, by William Hondius, 1629; and Elizabeth, by ditto, 1630, richly decorated with pearls—*very fine and rare*

48 Two—Frederick Henry, æt. 15, by Delff, 1629; and Charles Lewis, æt. 16, by ditto, 1634, ditto, ditto

49 Two—Frederick, King of Bohemia, by Delff, 1622; and Elizabeth, by R. Voerst, 1631, *Londini*, ditto

50 One—ELIZABETH, A THREE QUARTER, SUPERBLY DRESSED, after Mirevelt, by B. Bolſwert, 1615, from the Fothergill collection—FINE AND RARE

51 Two—Frederick V. and Elizabeth, half lengths, from ditto, by John Eillart Friſius—*rare*

52 One—KING AND QUEEN OF BOHEMIA, WITH ELEVEN CHILDREN, BY VISCHER, ditto

53 Two—DITTO, AND FIVE CHILDREN, BY WM PASS, WITH THIRTY-TWO ENGLISH VERSES, 1621, EXTRA FINE AND RARE; THE SAME PLATE, WITH THE ADDITION OF FIVE CHILDREN, THE YOUNGEST IN A CRADLE

54 One—DITTO, WITH ELEVEN CHILDREN, BY VISCHER, THE LARGE PRINT, WITH A VIEW OF HYDELBERG IN THE DISTANCE, SIXTEEN DUTCH VERSES—VERY RARE

55 One—DITTO, SITTING UNDER A TREE, WITH FOUR CHILDREN, THE YOUNGEST PLAYING WITH A RABBET—FINE AND RARE

56 One—DITTO, DITTO

57 One—THE PALATINE AND NASSAU FAMILY, by FRANCIS BRUN, 1627, on two ſheets—*very rare and fine*

POLITICALS, &c.

59 A large parcel ſatyrical

60 A ditto, political—time of Sir Robert Walpole, &c.

61 A ditto, political

DRAWINGS, &c.

62 Two—Henry IV. of France, 1610; and the Duc de Sully

63 Six—Madams la Bonde, de Cannauattot, de Chaſteauneuf, de Forigni, de Laube-Eſpine, de Luce—Par Queſnel

64 One—Sir Harbottle Grimſtone, maſter of the rolls, by S. Harding

65 One—Hugh Peters, in India ink

66 Eleven—of Saints, on vellum

*66 One—Sir William Berkely

67 Ten—Portraits of the Grand Moguls, in high preſervation, from the collection of the late Governor, Hollwell

68 Twenty-three—India drawings of the ſilk manufactory, ditto

69 Twenty-three—ditto, repreſenting the rice harveſt, &c. ditto, from the collection of Doctor Monro

*69 —ORIENAL MYTHOLOGY, THEIR IDEAS OF FUTURE REWARDS AND PUNISHMENTS, ON 48 ORIGINAL DRAWINGS, with explanations in the Chineſe and French languages, in the original binding —*curious*

70 Ten—Views in Rome, coloured

71 Nine—ditto ditto

72 Ten—ditto ditto

73 Four—for Cook's voyages, by Webber—*very fine*

74 Four—ditto ditto

75 Four—ditto ditto

76 Four—ditto ditto

77 Two—Views, from Hacket, by Denker, &c.

ENGLISH ENGRAVED PORTRAITS.

Q

78 Two—James, Duke of Queensberry, by L. du Guernier—*a sheet, very rare*; and F. Quarles

R

79 Seven—various, Richard I. II. and III.

80 Three—Christopher Rawlinson, æt. 55, 1733; Allan Ramsey, by Bickham; and Thomas Rowney, by J. Green

81 Six—A. Rathborne, 1616; Jer. Rich, 1659; Lewis Roberts, by Glover, 1637; William Rowland, &c.

82 Four—Sir George Rawdon, by R. White; Judge Rolle, by A. Hertoche—*fine*; Paul Rycaut, by R. White, &c.

83 Five—Christian Ravius, æt. 32; Con Ruton, by Coelmans; A. Rivet, by Meurs; John Riolans, by Lasne, &c.

84 Twelve—Thanes Autographs, &c.

85 Three—William Ramsey, sitting, by William Sherwin; a ditto, in a velvet cap, æt. 42; a ditto, a bust, æt. 24, by Cross—*fine*

86 One—The Rawlinson family, by Nutting, from the Fothergill collection—VERY FINE

87 Two—Jeremiah Rich, æt. 24, in an oval, four English verses; one ditto, in a square, left arm on a table, six English verses, by T. Cross—*fine and rare*

88 Two—Nathaniel Richards, by T. R.—*fine and rare*; with the copy

89 One—FRANCES, DUCHESS OF RICHMOND, quarto, by F. Delaram, 1623—*ſcarce*

90 One—Mark Ridley, M. D. by Elſtracke—*very rare*

91 Five—Sir Matthew White Ridley, 1788, by J. Fittler, &c.

92 One—Andreas Rivetus, by C. Van Dalen, æt. 60, the age was afterwards altered to 70

ENGLISH MEZZOTINTO PORTRAITS.

R

93 One—Lady Mary Radclyffe, in a dreſs of Oſtrich feathers, &c. whole length, by B. Lens—RARE AND FINE

94 One—John, Earl of Radnor, 1683, R. White, excudit—DITTO

95 Two—Daniel Race, 1772, by James Watſon—*proof*; and Hector Roſe, Eſq. by Val. Green

96 One—Thomas Raikes, Eſq. by C. H. Hodges—*private plate*

97 One—Miſs Martha Ray, by Val Green—*the large plate proof*

98 Three—Sir Thomas Reeve, by Bockman; Sir James Reynolds, 1747, by Faber, and Sir Dudley Ryder, whole length, by ditto

99 One—Iſaac Read, after Romney, by William Dickenſon—*proof*—*private plate*

100 One—Mr. Reddiſh, as poſthumus, whole length, by V. Green—*proof*

101 Three—Sir William Read, by Faithorne; Carolus Reinſenus, by G. White; and John Rudge, Eſq. by J. Faber, 1740

102 Four—Carolus Reinſenus, by White; Rembrandt, by Van Bleeck, 1747; William Richards, by Smith; and Abel Roper, by G. White

103 Two—Charles, Duke of Richmond, in robes of the garter, by J. Faber; and Charles, Duke of Richmond, profile, reading, after Romney, by James Watſon 1782

Fourteenth Day's Sale.

ENGLISH ENGRAVED PORTRAITS.

R CONTINUED

1 SIX—Sir Walter Ralegh; the family of Sir Thomas Remington, 1647—*private plate*—by G. Halfpenny, &c.

2 Three—Andreas Rivetus, by ditto, æt. 70; a ditto, æt. 78, 1650, by Meurs; and the Emperor Rodolphus, in a car with four horſes, by L. Kilian, 1627

3 One—JOHN, EARL OF ROCHESTER, by R. White, 1681—*very rare and fine*

4 One—James Roelans, by P. Pontius—*very fine*

5 Three—J. B. Rouſſeau, by J. Daulle; P. Rolli, by Wagner; and Antonio Rodil, by G. Vitalba

6 One—P. P. Rubens, with his hat, by Paul Pontius—VERY FINE

7 Two—P. Rubens, F. Rubens, Lepſius and Grotius, and child of Rubens, ſitting in a chair, by Salvador

8 One—PRINCE RUPERT, by A. BLOTELING, 1673—FINE AND RARE

9 One—ditto, by R. White—*proof*, ditto

10 Two—Admiral Ruyter, by John Viſscher, ſheet; a ditto, by A. Bloteling, quarto, with cannon, &c.

11 One—The Right Hon. Edward Ruſſel, Admiral, by William Elder—*fine and rare*

12 Two—Francis, Earl of Rutland, with collar of the garter—*fine and rare*; and the copy

CLERGY.

R

13 Six—W. Raſtall—*a proof*; James Relly, by S. Harding; Thomas Ridgley, by John Vandergucht—*proof*; Robert Robinſon, by Trotter; Romaine, &c.

14 Five—Edward Rainbow, æt. 74, by Sturt, ſix verſes; John Rawlet, æt. 44, by R. White; Edward Reynolds, by D. Loggan, folio; one ditto, by R. White, octavo; and Thomas de Rotheram, by Nugent

15 Five—Edward Reynolds, by D. Loggan; F. Roberts, æt. 40, 1648, by T. Croſs; Alexander Roſs, by Lombart, &c.

16 Four—Cardinal de Retz, by Morin; two ditto, quarto; Cardinal Roſſetti—*the original print*

17 Three—F. Roberts, æt. 40, 1648, by Croſs; Richard Rogers, in an oval; ditto, æt. 65, in a ſquare—*fine and ſcarce*

18 One—Henry Robinſon, biſhop of Carliſle—from a monumental plate—*rare*

AFTER SIR JOSHUA REYNOLDS.

19 Two—Sir Jeffery Amherſt, by J. Watſon; and Lord Anſon, by M'Ardel

20 One—The Ducheſs of Ancaſter, by J. Dixon, whole length—*proof*

21 One—John Aſh, M. D. whole length, by F. Bartolozzi—*proof*

22 One—Louiſa Counteſs of Aylesford, by V. Green—*ditto*

23 Three—Mary, Ducheſs of Ancaſter, 1756, in a circle, by R. Houſton; ditto—*a proof*; and Elizabeth, Counteſs Berkley, by M'Ardel

24 Two—William, Earl of Bath, by M'Ardel, 1758; and Joſeph Banks, Eſq. by Dickenſon

25 Two—Joſeph Baretti, by J. Watts; and James Boſwell, Eſq. by John Jones

26 One—The Duke of Bedford, in the character of St. George, and his brothers, by V. Green—*proof*

27 Two—Louis, Comte de Barbiano, by J. R. Smith, 1779; and Sir Walter Blackett, by Fittler

28 One—Admiral Boſcawen, whole length, by J. M'Ardel, 1757—*ſcarce*

29 Four—Miſs Boſville, by James Watſon; Mrs. Bonfoy, by Purcell; Mrs. Bouverie and Mrs. Crewe—*proof*; and Mrs. Bunbury, by James Watſon

30 Two—Lord Camden, whole length, by James Baſire, 1766; a ditto, by Haid—*proof*

31 Two—Miſs Campbell, by V. Green—*proof*; and Caroline, Counteſs Carliſle, by Watſon

32 One—Diana, Viſcounteſs Croſbie, whole length, by W. Dickenſon

33 Three—Lord John Cavendiſh, by J. Grozer—*proof*; Lord Richard Cavendiſh, by J. R. Smith; and George Seymour Conway, by Fiſher

34 One—Sir William Chambers, by V. Green—*proof*, *ſcarce*

35 One—The Honourable Francis Charteris, Eſq. by R. Houſton—*ſcarce*

36 Three—Nathaniel Chauncey, by Caroline Watſon, the ſquare plate; the ſame in an oval; and the copy

37 One—Lady Cockburne, with her three children, by Charles Wilkins—*proof*

38 One—Lady Elizabeth Compton, by V. Green, whole length—*proof*

39 Two—James Cholmondeley, by J. Jones—*proof*; and William, Duke of Cumberland, by Charles Spooner

40 Two—Lady Ann Dawſon, by M'Ardel; and Lord Dalkeith, by V. Green—*proofs*

41 One—Lady Betty Delmé, and children, by V. Green, whole length—*proof*

42 One—Elizabeth, Counteſs of Derby, by William Dickenſon, whole length—*fine*

43 One—Georgiana, Ducheſs of Devonſhire, by V. Green, Ditto—*proof*

44 Two—William, Duke of Devonſhire, 1755, by J. Faber; and the Hon. Richard Edgecumbe, by W. Dickenſon

45 Two—Lady Fennoulet, by M'Ardel; and Lady Forteſcue, 1757, by ditto

46 One—the Hon. Charles James Fox, with Lady Sarah Lenox, &c. by J. Watſon—*proof, ſcarce*

47 One—THE HON. CHARES JAMES FOX, by J. Jones, 1784—PROOF, SCARCE

48 One—GARRICK, BETWEEN TRAGEDY AND COMEDY, by V. Green—PROOF

49 Two—Mr. John Gawler, by J. R. Smith; and the ſons of ditto, by ditto—*proof*

50 Two—Lord George Germain, by M'Ardel; and the Marquis of Granby, by R. Houſton—*proofs*

51 One—Marquis of Granby, ſtanding, with his horſe, by J. Watſon—*fine*

52 Two—ditto, by Richard Houſton, 1760; and Earl Gower, by E. Fiſher, 1765

53 Two—Lord Grantham, and brothers, by Cheeſman; and Lord Melburne's children, by F. Bartolozzi—*proofs*

54 One—Sir William Hamilton, by H. Hudſon, whole length—*proof*

55 One—Jane, Counteſs of Harrington, by V. Green,

56 One—Lady Harriot Herbert, by V. Green—*proof*

57 One—Admiral Auguſtus Hervey, by Fiſher—*proof* whole length—*proof*

58 Two—ditto; and Lady Caroline Howard, by ditto—*proofs*

59 Three—John Hawkeſworth, by J. Watſon; Maſter Henry Hoare, by Wilken; and Sir Abraham Hume—*proof*

60 Two—Admiral Lord Hood, by J. Jones; and Sir Wm. Hamilton, by H. Hudſon

61 One—Sir Edward Hughes, whole length, by J. Jones—*proof*

62 One—John Hely Hutchinſon, by James Watſon

63 Two—Lady Mary Kent, by J. Dean; and Emily, Counteſs of Kildare, 1754, by M'Ardell

64 Two—the Hon. Auguſtus Keppel, by E. Fiſher, 1759, whole length; and Wm. Kingſley, by R. Houſton, 1760

65 One—William, Duke of Leinſter, by John Dixon—*fine proof*

66 One—John, Lord Viſcount Ligonier, on horſeback, by E. Fiſher

67 Two—John Lockhart, Eſq. by M'Ardel—*one a touched proof*

68 One—Biſhop Markham, by J. R. Smith—*fine and ſcarce*

69 Two—Rev. William Maſon, by Doughty; and Mrs. Montagu, by J. R. Smith

70 Three—Thomas Newton, Biſhop of Briſtol, by T. Watſon, *proof*; and the Duke and Ducheſs of Northumberland, by E. Fiſher

71 Two—Miſs O'Brien, by C. Phillips, *proof*; and Omai, by John Jacobi, whole length

72 One—Duke of Orleans, by J. R. Smith, whole length—*proof*

73 One—Miſs Palmer, by ditto—*proof*

74 One—William, Duke of Portland, by John Murphy—*proof*

75 One—Percival Pott, Eſq. by Chas. Townley—SCARCE

76 Two—Sir Joſhua Reynolds, by ditto; and one, by Caroline Kirkley

77 One—John Reynolds, S. T. B. 1757, the Uncle of Sir Joſhua, by J. M'Ardell — *old impreſſion, fine and ſcarce*

78 Two—Biſhop Robinſon, by J. R. Smith; and John, Earl of Rothes, by M'Ardell

79 Two—Charles, Marquis of Rockingham; and Robert, Lord Romney, by Fiſher aud Finlayſon, whole lengths

80 One—Mary Iſabella, Ducheſs of Rutland, by V. Green, whole length—*proof*

81 One—ditto, by J. K. Sherwin

82 One—Charles, Duke of Rutland, by W. Dickinſon, whole length—*proof*

83 One—E. M. Counteſs of Saliſbury, by V. Green, whole length—*proof*

84 One—Sir Charles Saunders, by M'Ardell—*proof*

85 Two—Prince Serge Gallitzen, and Princeſs Barbara, with their ſon, by Caroline Watſon—*one a proof*

86 Two—Biſhop Shipley, by Trotter; ditto, by J. R. Smith

87 One—Mrs. Siddons, as the Tragic Muſe, by Francis Haward—FIRST STATE OF THE FINISHED PROOF, VERY RARE

88 Two—Lady Charles Spencer, by W. Dickinſon; and Lord Henry and Lady Charlotte Spencer, by J. Jones

89 One—Lady Charlotte Talbot, by V. Green, whole length—*proof*

90 One—Francis, Marquis of Taviſtock, by James Watſon—PROOF

91 One—Richard, Earl Temple, by W. Dickinſon —*fine proof*

92 One—Thomas, Biſhop of Rocheſter, by Thomas Park

93 One—Col. Henry Townſhend, by J. M'Ardell—*rare*

94 One—Ann, Viſcounteſs Townſhend, by V. Green, whole length—*proof*

95 One—ditto, with the Hon. Mrs. Beresford, and Mrs. Gardiner, by T. Watſon—*firſt impreſſion, fine*

96 One—the three Lady Waldegraves, by V. Green—*proof, ſcarce*

97 Two—Maria, Counteſs Waldegrave, by M'Ardell, *a proof*; and an etching, by Hoare—*ſcarce*

98 One—George, Prince of Wales, by Francis Haward—*fine*

99 One—THE ETCHING OF DITTO—RARE

100 Two—Caleb Whitefoord, Eſq. by J. Jones; W. Windham

101 Two—the Rev. Thomas Warton, by C. Hodges; and Harry Woodward, by James Watſon

Fifteenth Day's Sale.

FOREIGN PORTRAITS.

R

1 SIX—G. N. la Reynie, by Van Schuppen, 1665; Lewis Requeſens, &c.

2 Seven—Rabelais, by Habert; Francis Rivera, by Mallery, &c.

3 Three—Robertus Secouſſe, by J. Andran; Renaudot, by F. Chereau; and Antoine de la Roque, by Lepice

4 Four—Raphael, by P. Pontius; a ditto, by J. Freii; Rigaud, by Daullé; and Ronchalis

ENGLISH MEZZOTINTO PORTRAITS.

CONTINUED.

R

5 One—Frances Thereſa, Ducheſs of Richmond, whole length, after H. Gaſcar—*very rare*

6 Two—Charles, Duke of Richmond, with a hound, ſmall whole length, by J. Becket; a ditto, in a ſmall oval, ſtar and ribbon, J. Becket, ex.—*ſcarce*

7 Two—Charles, Duke of Richmond, by J. Watſon; and William, Earl of Rochford, by V. Green—*proofs*

8 One—Admiral Lord Bridges Rodney, by Val. Green *proof*

9 One—ditto, whole length, by T. Gainſborough du Pont—*proof*

10 One—Nicolas Rowe, Eſq. P. L.—*fine*

11 Two—John, Duke of Roxburghe, in robes of the garter, by Faber, 1741; and Robert, Duke of Roxburghe, by M'Ardell, 1755—*private plates*

12 One—Rubens, with his wife and child, by M'Ardell—*very fine*

13 One—Rubens and family, after Jordans, from the Houghton collection—*ditto*

14 One—Ruben's Wife, by Richard Earlom—*fine*

15 One—the children of Rubens, by Taſſaert—*proof*

16 One—Prince Rupert, after Rembrandt, by V. Green—*proof*

17 One—Wriotherley, Lord Ruſſell, when young, whole length, J. Becket, ex.—*fine and rare*

18 One—John, Duke of Rutland, whole length, in his robes, after Jervas, by Faber—*ſcarce*

19 Three—General Richmond, alias Webb, by J Faber; Admiral William Rowley, by ditto, 1745; and Admiral de Ruyter, by J. Van Somer

CLERGY.

20 Three—Joſhua Richardſon, by Faber; Samuel Roſewell, by ditto; in an oval, quarto; and John Rhudde, by W. Dickenſon—*a proof*

ENGLISH MEZZOTINTO PORTRAITS.

S

21 Three—Madam Philadelphia Saunders, by A. Browne; Katherine Sidley, by R. Thompſon, folio; and Jane Roberts, by A. Brown—*a reverſe*

22 Three—Madam Katherine Sidley, in an ovol, quarto, by R. Williams; Harvey, Counteſs of Stamford, in a ſquare, by R. Thompſon; and Mrs. Vaillant, hand on a flower-pot, by W. Vaillant

23 Four—Lady Helena Rawdon, by Brooks; Sally Saliſbury; Maria, Viſcounteſs Sarsfield, by V. Green; and Griſelda, Counteſs Stanhope, by M'Ardell

24 Four—Nicolas Sanderſon—*proof*; Francis Smith, architect, by Vanhacken; Sir Hans Sloane, by Faber; and Ezekiel Spanheim, 1707, by Simon

25 Five—Anthony Sayer, grand maſter of maſons, by Faber; F. B. Seneſino, by Alexander Vanhaaken, 1735; John Sturges—*proof*; Owen M'Swiny, by Van Bleeck, 1749, &c.

26 Three—Joſeph Sabine, 1739, by Faber; John, Earl of Stair, by ditto; and General James Stanhope, by Simon

27 Three—Sir Edwyn Sandys, by V. Green; Lord Henry Scot, by W. Faithorne; James, Lord Stanhope, by Simon; and Charles, Duke of Somerſet, by Faber, 1714

28 Three—Admiral Charles Stewart, 1740, by Faber; John, Earl of Sandwich, by V. Green, 1774; and Sir Charles Saxton, by S. W. Reynolds

29 Three—Madam Soams, by Becket; Mrs. Diana Turnor, by ditto; and Anne, Counteſs of Yarmouth, by G. de Koning, ſix verſes

30 Three—Sir John Salter, lord mayor of London, 1740, by A. Miller; W. Saunders, M. D. by Charles Townley, 1792; and Edward Smyth, M. D. 1779, by V. Green—*proof*

31 Two—Shakeſpeare, by J. Simon; and Thomas Sutton, founder of the Charter-houſe, whole length, by Faber, 1754

32 Two—Henry Sidney, with a dog, by Alexander Browne; and Lords John and Bernard Stuarts, by Thompſon

33 Two—William Shirley, Eſq. by M'Ardell; and John, Earl of Stair, by T. Burford

34 Two—Sir Cloudeſly Shovel, in armour, in an oval—*proof*; and Sir Edward Sprague, admiral, 1672, *ſcarce*

35 One—the Hon. Henry Singleton, whole length, by Brooks

36 Two—Samuel Smith, Eſq. and Madam Smith, by G. White—*ſcarce*

37 Two—John Sommers, by Faber, 1733; and Charles, Duke of Somerſet, by Simon

38 Three—Edward Spry, æt. 57, 1785; John Spry, æt. 18, 1783; and the tyler of a masonic Lodge, by J. Jehner—*scarce*

39 Two—Edward Spry, æt. 90, 1785, ship-wright, at Plymouth; and Edward Spry, æt. 57, 1785—*a proof, rare*

40 One—Harvey, Countess Stamford, by R. Tompson—*fine proof*

41 Two—John Stacpoole, Esq. 1771; and Sir Richard Stacpoole, by James Watson—*scarce*

42 Two—Griselda, Countess Stanhope, by M'Ardell; and Maria, Countess of Suffolk—*proof, rare*

43 One—John Swan, Esq. by V. Green—*ditto*

44 Three—Miss Charlotte Spencer, Miss Stuart, and Miss Thellusson, by V. Green—*proofs*

CLERGY.

45 Two—Timothy Rogers, quarto, by B. Williams; and Joseph Standen, in an oval, large quarto, after J. Wills—*scarce*

46 Five—Bishops—Stapledon, by Faber; Sherlock, by M'Ardell, 1757; Arthur Smyth, 1771, by James Watson; John Sterne, by T. Beard; and Thomas Strickland, by Faber

47 Four—Sacheverell, by Johnston; Dr. Sharp, by V. Green; Mr. Shirley, by J. Dixon; and John Shower, V. D. M. æt. 52, 1709, in an oval, by J. Faber

ENGLISH ENGRAVED PORTRAITS.

S

48 Ten—various, by Dalton, &c.

49 Sixteen—ditto, by Thane

50 Seven—Salmon, by Sherwin—*fine*; ditto, æt. 43, 1687, by R. White, &c.

51 Two—Richard Saunders, in an oval; one in a ſquare, by Ord, 1613, ſix Engliſh verſes

52 Sixteen—Thanes autographs, &c.

53 Three—Jacobi Sachs, with curious emblems, 1661; Chriſtopher Schwaiger, by L. Kilian, 1600; and John Jac Scheuchzerus, 1672, by J. Nutting, London

54 Three—Thomas Skelton—*fine*; John Sleidan; and Andrew Snape, by R. White

55 Six—Lord Somers, Earl of Sunderland, by Houbraken; the Earl of Scarborough, by Hall, &c.

56 Five—writing-maſters—J. Sealy, John Seddon, by Sturt; G. Shelly, by Bickhams; Charles Snell, by Elder; and John Smith, by Vanderbanc

57 Six—modern portraits—Princeſs Sophia, by Caroline Watſon; daughters of the Counteſs Spencer; Lady Sefton; Mrs. Siddons, by J. K. Sherwin, &c.

58 Eight—N. Saunderſon, by V. Gucht; Robert Simſon, M. D. by A. Baillie, 1776; Eben. Sibly, &c.

59 Four—Mr. Savage, by M. V. Gucht; Joſhua Peart Scroope; James Smith, eye-maker, by J. Pine, 1717; and Mr. John Stanley

60 One—Baron Saley, 1617, by Simon Paſſe—*fine and rare*

61 Two—Thomas Sanders, of Ireton, by D. Loggan; and Anton Sherley, by Sadeler

62 Two—Edward, Earl of Sandwich, in an oval, by A. Bloteling; and one ditto, ſquare, by ditto

63 One—Sir George Savile, by Wilſon and Baſire—BEFORE THE LIGHT IN THE WINDOW

64 Two—Frederick, Duke Schonberg, by P. Vandrebanc, ſheet; and one ditto, oval, by S. Gribelin, 1689

65 One—THE GENEALOGIE OF THE SCOTISH KINGS, FROM MARGARET, MARRIED TO MALCOLME III. AND FROM MARGARET, DAUGHTER TO HENRY VII. MARRIED TO JAMES IV. WITH THEIR PORTRAITS—VERY RARE AND CURIOUS

66 One—Anthony, Earl of Shafteſbury, by R. White, 1680—*fine*

67 Two—ditto, and one from Gillam

68 One—ditto, 1673, by A. BLOTELING—VERY FINE AND RARE

69 Two—Shakeſpeare—*proofs on India paper*, by T. Trotter, 1794

70 One—ditto, by Godefroy, 1796—*proof*

71 One—DITTO, by MARTIN DROSHOUT

72 One—John Talbot, Earl of Shrewſbury

73 Two—Siameſe, ambaſſador and prieſt, after Rubens, by W. Baillie—*fine*

74 One—Siameſe, ambaſſador, 1686, by Hainzelman—*rare and curious*

75 Two—Sir Philip Sidney; and Maria Sidney, Counteſs of Pembroke, by Courbes—*fine and ſcarce*

76 Four—Sir P. Sidney, 1586, by Elstrache; Al. Sidney, folio; and two ditto, by Jackson—*one unfinished*

77 Two—John, Earl of Somerset, time of Richard II. and ditto, time of Henry VI.—*rare and curious*

78 One—Christopher Simpson, playing on the viola di gambo—*rare*

79 One—PAUL VAN SOMER—PROOF, VERY RARE

80 One—Henry, Earl of Southampton, by Simon Passe, 1617—*fine and rare*

81 Three—Fred. Spanheim, 1683, by A. de Blois; one ditto, by C. Van Dalen, 1644; and Ez. Spanheim, 1702, by R. White

82 One—ROBERT STAFFORD, BY D. LOGGAN—PROOF BEFORE NAME OF ENGRAVER, &c. — VERY RARE

83 One—Lady Stanhope, by Basire, 1772

84 One—Stanislaus, King of Poland, by A. Fogg, 1793 —*proof*

85 Two—Robert Stapleton, by Marshall, &c. James Shirley, by Marshall, 1646

86 Two—James Sylvester, by Van Dalen; and Robert Stapleton, by Lombart, folio

87 One—John Starter, an oval, drawn by swans—*rare*

88 Two—Henry, Earl of Stamford; Thos. Earl of Strafford, by Simmoneau—*proof*

89 One—a ditto, by P. Huybrecht—*fine and scarce*

90 One—Thomas Street, by R. White, 1688—*ditto*

91 One—Thomas, Earl of Suffolk, with the staff of lord-treasurer, by R. Elstrake—*very fine and rare*

CLERGY.

92 Six—Samuel Say, 1743, by J. Hall; James Seed, Thomas Sharp, æt. 56, by Aliamet; Samuel Stennett, by Holloway; Joſeph Stennett, by William Walker; P. Stockdale

93 Six—John Scott, by M. Vandergucht, folio; Henry Scougal, by Trotter; Thomas Shaw, by J. Green; John Shower, 1714, by Drapenier; Samuel Slater, by R. White, 1692; and George Stradling, by R. White

94 Ten—various, Biſhop Sandes, &c.

95 Seven—Biſhops—Sancroft, by Elder, octavo; R. Sanderſon, 1662, by W. Dolle; ditto, æt. 76, by R. White, octavo; Scroop, by Harding; J. Sharpe, 1679, by G. Vertue; and Sheldon, by Gardiner

96 Three—Sancroft, by D. Loggan, 1680, folio; Sanderſon, 1662, by W. Dolle; and Sheldon, by Clamp

97 One—Biſhop Seabury, by W. Sharp, 1786—*proof*

98 Three—William Sherwin, æt. 65, 1672, by William Sherwin, jun.; Joſ. Shute, 1643, by W. Marſhall, folio, twenty Latin and Engliſh lines; and Cuth. Sidenham, æt. 31, 1654, by R. Gaywood, 1654—*fine and ſcarce*

99 Four—Ric. Sibbs, æt. 58, quarto; a ditto, 12mo. by William Marſhall; Cuth. Sidenham, by Gaywood, 1654; and Edward Simſon, æt. 73, eight Latin verſes —*ditto*

100 Five—Henry Smith, by Croſs; Benjamin Spencer, by ditto; Richard Stock, by T. Rawlins, eight Engliſh verſes; a ditto, by Jenner, four Engliſh verſes, &c.

101 Four—JOHN DUNN, Scotus, by Cheaveau, in an oval of roses; a ditto, with spectacles, reading a book, an etching; Thomas Scott, æt. 45, 1624, by C. Pass; and Richard Stock, by Jenner—*ditto*

102 One—BISHOP THOMAS STRICKLAND, by Tomasin, folio—*very rare*

Sixteenth Day's Sale.

BY J. SMITH.

1 ONE—ROBERT, EARL OF AYLESBURY, WITH THE STAFF OF LORD CHAMBERLAIN—PROOF, VERY RARE

2 Four—Chr. Duke of Albemarle; Arnold, ditto; G. Earl of Athlone; and Henry D'Auverquerk—*fine*

3 Four—A. Earl of Albemarle; G. Earl of Athlone; H. D'Auverquerk; and Madame ditto

4 Three—Queen Ann and Princeſs Ann

*4 Four—ditto

5 One—WILLIAM ANSTRUTHER, of Anſtruther, after J. B. de Medina—FINE AND RARE

6 Three—Addiſon; Boyle; and John, Duke of Buckingham—*proof*

7 One—JOHANNES BAGGERUS, after Saleman — FINE AND RARE

8 Two—Sir John Bowyer; and John, Earl of Bridgwater—*fine and rare*

9 Two—John, Marquis of Blandford, *proof*; and John, Lord Burleigh, with a gun

10 Two—Duchefs of Bolton, *proof*; and Lady Brownlowe, whole length—*fine*

11 Three—Duchefs of Bolton; Lord Buckhurft, with his fifter Mary, and Lady Brandon

12 Four—John, Earl of Bridgwater; George, Prince of Brunfwick; Sir Thomas Bury and Lord Bury—*fine*

13 Three—John, Earl of Bridgwater; the Hon. William Bromley; and Gilbert Burnet—*fine*

14 Four—Queen Caroline, the Duchefs of Cleveland, and Prifcilla Cooper

15 Two—Robert Cecil, and Sir John Crifp—*proofs*

16 Three—the Hon. William Cecil, whole length; Cofimas; and William, Duke of Cumberland—*fine*

17 Two—Sir Robert Clayton, and Lord William Cowper—*fine*

18 Three—Lady Carteret, Lord Churchill's daughter, and Lady Elizabeth Cromwell

19 Three—Robert Cecil; F. Cornaro; and William, Duke of Cumberland—*proofs*

20 Five—two of Charles I. two of Charles II. and one of Queen Caroline

21 Four—Charles III. of Spain; Charles XI. and XII. of Sweden; and John Cornelius, Doge of Venice—*fine*

22 Four—Mrs. Carter, Mrs. Chichely, Lady Copley, and Mrs. Elinor Copley—*fine*

23 Two—Thomas Colefon, Efq. and Mitford Crowe—*fine and rare*

24 Two—Richard, Lord Clifford; with Lady Jane, and Lady Elizabeth Cromwell, whole lengths—*fine*

25 Two—Lady Copley and Lady Cromwell—*proofs*
26 Two—Sir Robert Cotton and Thomas Coulſon—*proofs, ſcarce*
27 Three—Sir Robert Clayton; William, Lord Cowper; and William Cowper, ſurgeon
28 One—Crawford, of Kilbirny, after J. B. Medino, with armorial bearings—*fine and rare*
29 One—ELIZABETH, LADY CUTTS, after G. Kneller, 1698—FINE AND RARE
30 Two—Madam Davenant and the Counteſs of Dorcheſter—*fine*
31 One—LADY MARY DOUGLAS—*fine and rare*
32 Three—William Dolben, *a proof*; Charles, Earl of Dorſet; and Mary, Counteſs of Eſſex
33 Four—Prince Eugene; Mary, Counteſs of Eſſex; Charles, Lord Euſton; and John, Earl of Exeter
34 Four—three of Frederick, King of Pruſſia, *one a proof*, and Prince Frederick
35 Four—William Fellowes; Biſhop Fowler; Gunning, Biſhop of Ely, *ſcarce*; and Martin Folkes, in a cap, 1719
36 Seven—George I.—the ſecond two as Prince of Wales and George Elector of Brunſwick
37 Four—three of George Prince of Denmark; and Sidney, Earl of Godolphin
38 Four—George, Prince of Denmark; Count Gallas; and George of Heſſe-Caſſel
39 Four—George of Denmark, Mr. and Mrs. Gibbons, and the Ducheſs of Grafton
40 Four—Samuel Garth; Grinlin Gibbons, one with his wife; and Sir Richard Gipps
41 One—David Boyle, Earl of Glaſgow—*fine and ſcarce*
42 One—ditto, *ditto*

43 Two—William, Duke of Gloucester, with the flower-pot, *very fine*; and one with Mr. Benjamin Bathhurst—*proof*

44 Four—William, Duke of Gloucester

45 Two—Sir Henry and Lady Mary Goodricke, in ovals —*rare*

46 Two—Lady Helen Hamilton, *proof*; and the Ladies Henrietta and Katherine Hide—*fine*

47 Two—Thomas, Earl of Haddington; and Sir William Hodges—FINE AND SCARCE

48 Four—Anthony Henly; Lord Hinchinbrook; Abraham Hondius; and Mrs. Arabella Hunt

49 Four—Mrs. Conway Hackett; Mrs. Rachel How; Lady Howard, whole length, standing; and Mrs. Arabella Hunt

50 Six—James I. and II.

51 Five—Queen Katharine, Lady Grisell Karr, Mrs. Anne Killigrew, and Ann Kynnesman—*fine*

52 Two—John Kettlewell, and Thomas Knipe — VERY FINE

53 Two—ELIZABETH, COUNTESS OF KILDARE—*fine and rare*

54 Three—two of Kneller, and Devereux Knightley

55 Two—JOHN LAMBERT, Esq. and Sir P. Lilly—FINE and RARE

56 Four—Anthony Leigh, Lewis XIV. John Locke, and Madam Loftus

57 Two—John, Earl of Mar, sheet; and John, Earl of Mulgrave

58 Four—Joseph Martyn, merchant; General Thomas Maxwell; Henry, Lord Delámar; and John, Earl of Mulgrave

59 Five—Madam Dorothy Mafon; Sarah, Duchefs of Marlborough; and three of Queen Mary

60 One—QUEEN MARY, WITH A HIGH HEAD-DRESS, after Vander Vaart—*fine and fcarce*

61 Three—Mary of Efte, *one a proof*; Mary II.; cenotaph of ditto, *a proof*

62 Three—Sarah, Duchefs of Marlborough; Michael de Molinos; and Ann, Duchefs of Monmouth, with her fons

63 Five—Duke and Duchefs of Marlborough; and James, Duke of Monmouth

64 Three—Charles Napier, Efq.; Thomas, Duke of Newcaftle; and Sir Ifaac Newton—*fine*

65 Three—James, Duke of Ormond, a fquare; one ditto, oval; and Mary, Duchefs of Ormond, whole length —*fine*

66 Three—Charles Napier; Mary, Duchefs of Ormond, whole length; and Robert, Earl of Oxford

67 Three—Thomas, Earl of Pembroke; the Old Pretender, and his fifter, after Largilliere; and one on a cufhion

68 Four—Sir William Petty; George Petty; Sir John Percival, whole length; and Alexander Pope—*fine*

69 Two—ROBERT, EARL OF ROXBURGH, æt. 19, 1696, after D. Pattin, RARE; and Lady Roxburgh, in an oval, after Kneller

N. B. This Print is ufually called Mrs. Morgan.

70 Three—Chriftopher Rawlinfon, of Lancafhire; Wm. Richards, and Captain Edward Rigby

71 Two—Laurence, Earl of Rochefter; and Sir George Rooke—*very fine and rare*

72 Four—Boyle, Countess of Ranelagh; Bessy, Countess of Rochford; Ann Roydhouse; and Catharine, Countess of Rutland—*fine*

73 Four—Diana, Duchess of St. Albans; Frances, Countess of Salisbury; Jane Skeffington; and Princess Sophia of Brunswick

74 Three—Henry Sacheverell; James, Earl of Salisbury; and Thomas Smith, Bishop of Carlisle—*fine*

75 One—JAMES, EARL OF SEAFIELD, with armorial bearings—FINE AND RARE

76 —Two—Duke of Schomberg, on horseback; and Sir Cloudesly Shovell—*very fine*

77 Two—a ditto; and Maynard, Count Schomberg

78 Six—The Honourable Mrs. Sherard; two—Sophia Dowager of Brunswick; and three—Sophia Dorothea of Prussia

79 Four—John Smith, Edward Southwell, C. W. Stockdale, and Thomas Tompson

80 Four—John, Lord Sommers; Sir Richard Steele, from Richardson; a ditto, from Kneller; and William Stukeley—*fine*

81 Three—John, Lord Sommers; Charles, Duke of Somerset; and C. W. Stockdale—*proofs*

82 One—GEORGE, VISCOUNT TARBAT, æt. 60, 1692—FINE AND RARE

83 Two—JOHN, MARQUIS OF TWEEDALE; ONE IN ERMINE—*fine and scarce*

84 Three—Thomas Tompion; Charles, Viscount Townshend, with a parrot; and Grevil Verney—*fine*

85 Three—Sir John Vanbrugh; Grevil Verney; and William, Lord Villers, with his sister Mary, whole length—*fine*

86 One—JOHANNES WITT, MERCHANT, 1704, after Warner Haſſell's—EXTRA RARE AND FINE

87 Four—Ann Warner; Thomas, Lord Wharton; Sir Chriſtopher Wren; and W. Wycherley—*fine*

88 Six—Ann Warner; Counteſs of Weſtmoreland; two Princeſs Wilhelmina; Lady Elizabeth Willmot; and Mrs. Yarborough

89 One—THE HONOURABLE Mrs. ANN WATSON—PROOF—VERY RARE AND FINE

90 Four—Thomas, Lord Wharton; Dudley Woodbridge; Henry Worſter; and Mr. William Woodward, after Taverner—*ſcarce*

91 Six—different, of William III.

92 One—JAMES, DUKE OF YORK, WITH THE ANCHOR—PROOF, *very fine and rare*

93 One—MARIA, DUCHESS OF YORK, ſold by R. Palmer, whole length—FINE AND RARE

Seventeenth Day's Sale.

FOREIGNERS.

S

1 NINE—P. Stockmans, by Harrewyn; Joseph Sebastion, by Habert, &c.

2 Ten—Peter Seguier, by Mellan; Anna, Duchess of Savoy; Spinola; Count de Soissons, by C. David, &c.

3 Five—Francis de Sales, by Morin; P. Sequin, by Pitau, 1664; D. Sanguin, by ditto, &c.

4 One—Marshal Saxe, by J. G. Will, 1748

5 Four—Spinola, by Muller; John, Duke of Saxony, by W. Hondius, 1628, a first impression; Victor, Duke Savoy, &c.

6 Six—Pope Sixtus V. F. de Sales, by Pitau, &c.

7 One—ADMIRAL STELLINGWERF, by Bloteling—VERY FINE

8 Six—Le Sueur, by Cochin, 1731; An Sacchi, by Vallet; Spranger, and his wife, by E. Sadeler; A. M. Schurman, by Van Dalen, &c.

9 One—Marquis Spinola, on horſeback, with Hen Vondenbergh, 1620, bordered with ſmall oval views of cities—*ſcarce*

T

10 Seven—J. de Thou, by Lochon; Seb. Truchet, by Thomaſſin; Chriſtopher de Thou, by Morin, &c.

11 Seven—J. de Thon, by Vonillemont; C. de Thou, by Morin; Taſſo, by Depuis, &c.

12 One—The Princeſs Troubetſkoy, by Daulle, 1761

13 One—L. A. COMTE DE TOULOUZE, by P. Drevet—VERY FINE

14 Five—F. de Troy, by Poilly; Titian, by Aug. Carraci; Anton Tempeſta, &c.

15 One—Titians's ſon and nurſe, after Titian, by Murphy—*proof*

ENGLISH ENGRAVED PORTRAITS.

T

16 Six—David la Touche, of Wicklow, by J. K. Sherwin, &c.

17 Four—John Taylor, by Van Hove; Thomas Tryon, by R. White; John Tutchin, by M. V. Gucht; and Sir John Trenehard, by Beſtland

18 Six—Portraits to illuſtrate Granger, &c.
19 One—George, Viscount Tarbat, 1692, by P. Vanderbank—fine and scarce
20 One—Susannah Temple, Lady Thornhurst, &c. 1620, by R. White, from the Fothergill collection—*ditto*
21 Two—Sir Peter and Lady Elinor Temple, by R. Gaywood, 1658—very rare and fine
22 Five—James Thompſon, by Baſire; Kellom Tomlinſon, by M. la Cave, 1754, &c.
23 Two—Caroline, Comteſſe de Thum, and Mrs. Tickell, by Condé
24 Five—George Trappe, by C. Knight, 1789; Sir John Trenchard, by Beſtland; Captain Richard Tyrrell, by Worlidge; Edward Thompſon, &c.
25 Four—Richard Tomlinſon, 1657, by T. Croſs; John Torrentius, 1628, by Holſtein—*fine*; Sir Henry Tyrrell, 1582, &c.
26 One—Sir George Treby, by R. White, 1694
27 One—Sir Thomas Trevor, by ditto, 1702—*fine*
28 Three—Martin Van Tromp, in an oval, æt. 54, 1648, after S. D. Vlieger, by C. Van Dalen; and two of Cornelius Tromp
29 One—Martin, and Cornelius Tromp, drawn in a car, by Concordia, &c. many emblems, Victoria, Vigilautia, &c. by J. Saenredam—a ſheet, *curious*
30 One—Cornelius Tromp, after P. Lely, by A. Bloteling, 1676—*fine old impreſſion*
31 One—ditto, ſtanding in armour, a black boy with a helmet, after Ferd, Bol. by Lambert Viſcher—a ſheet—*fine*
32 Two—Prince Henry Charles la Tremoille, knight of the garter, 1661, by P. Philippe; and Viſcount Turenne, by Nantueil

33 One—Sir James Turner, by R. White—*fine*

34 One—Sir John Turton, 1701, by W. Sherwin—*very rare and fine*

CLERGY.

35 Five—John Taylor, by Houbraken, 1754; James Townley, by Charles Townley, 1794; Joſeph Trapp, by Clamp; Richard Turner, by Stanier, 1787

36 Seven—Jer. Taylor, by Lombart; Thomas Taylor, æt. 56, in an oval, by Croſs, eight Engliſh verſes, &c.

37 Three—Thomas Taylor, æt. 56, by W. Marſhall, four Latin verſes; John Trapp, æt. 53, by R. Gaywood, 1654, ſix Engliſh verſes; and Anton. Tuckney, by R. White—*fine*

38 Two—Thomas Teniſon, by Vandrebanc, 1695; and one ditto, by R. White, folio

39 One—Thomas Teniſon, by Vandrebanc, 1695—*fine*

40 Three—Tillotſon, by A. Blooteling; ditto, by R. White, octavo; and Richard Trevor, æt. 64, 1771, by J. Collyer

ENGLISH MEZZOTINTO PORTRAITS.

T

41 One—Mr. Richard Tatterſall, by John Jones

42 Three—Charles, Lord Talbot, by Bockman; Richard, Earl Temple, by Houſton; and Sir William Thompſon, by J. Faber, 1739

43 Three—J—, Count de Tarouca, by Simon; C. Van Tromp, sold by Brown and Tenducie, by Finlayson —*the two last proofs*

44 Two—Pierce Tempest—*a proof*; and Richard Thompson, by Place—*scarce*

45 One—John Thornton, Esq. whole length, by V. Green—*proof*

46 One—Humphry French, the Good Lord Mayor—*scarce*

47 Three—Kirkes Townley, by Charles Townley; Timothy Treadway, by Faber; and William Tunstall, in quarto, three Latin lines

CLERGY.

48 Two—Bishop Talbot, 1721; and Trimnell, 1721—*scarce*

49 Four—Dr. Sharpe, by V. Green; Matthew Tindall, æt. 78, 1733, by J. Faber; Tillotson, by J. Simon; ditto, by Faber—*proof*

TOPOGRAPHICAL.

50 Bedfordshire—twelve, maps, plans, &c.

51 Berkshire—twenty ditto, view of Windsor-castle, Colshill, by Vertue, &c.

52 Buckinghamshire—twenty-one—Stow-gardens, &c.

53 Cambridgeshire—thirty—Cathedral Church of Ely, the Town of Wisbech, View of Cambridge, &c.

54 Cheshire—twenty-one—Eton-hall, on two sheets, by Toms; ditto, by Kip, maps, plans, &c.

55 Cumberland, &c.—ſeventeen—the Cathedral of Carliſle, by King; St. Michael's Mount, &c.

56 Devonſhire—fifteen—Plymouth-dock, maps, &c.

57 Dorſetſhire—thirty—from Hutchin's Hiſtory, &c.

*57 Thirteen—ditto

58 Durham—a Plan of the River Waer, from New Bridge to Sunderland-Bar, four ſheets, by Burleigh and Thompſon, 1737

59 A ditto, and twelve maps, &c.

60 Eſſex—ſix—a Plan of Luxbrogh and Cockſell's Farms, at Chigwell, drawn on vellum, 1727; the Earl of Tinley's, on two ſheets, by Roque, &c.

61 Hampſhire, &c.—eleven—Porcheſter-caſtle, &c.

62 Kent—View of Rocheſter, Chatham, and Sheerneſs, with the burning the Fleet, 1664, by R. de Hooge—*ſcarce*; Docks of Sheerneſs and Woolwich, &c.

63 Lancaſhire, &c.—ten—maps, &c.

64 London, &c.—nineteen—maps, plans of canals, &c.

65 ——— one—the Royal Fire-works, on the River Thames, before Whitehall, 1713, by B. Lens—*ſcarce*

66 ———five—the Fire of London, 1666, by W. Birch, &c.

67 ——— Views of Arundel-houſe, with portraits of the Earl of Arundel and family, publiſhed by Mr. Thane

68 Norfolk, &c.—a parcel

69 Oxfordſhire—eight

70 Rutlandſhire, &c.—fifteen

71 Somerſetſhire—ſeventeen

72 Staffordſhire, &c.—twenty

73 Surrey, &c.—twenty-five—views, &c.

74 Warwickshire—twenty—Plan of Coventry, View of St. Philip's Church, Birmingham, plans, &c.

75 Westmoreland and Wilts—fifteen—the large oak, Longleat, &c.

76 Worcestershire and Yorkshire—sixteen—Tong, Duncomb-park, &c.

77 Twenty Views from Harding's Shapespeare

78 Wales—a parcel

79 Scotland—fourteen—maps, &c.

80 Ireland—four—Views in Killarny, aquatint, by Alken

81 ——— twenty-five—the seige of Londonderry, &c.

82 Forty-two—Views, by Buck, selected for Clarendon's History of the Rebellion

83 Sixteen—Buck's Views

84 Two—Plan of the Camp at Lexdon, by Tinney; and a map of the Invasions of England and Ireland, with all their civil wars since the conquest—*scarce*

85 Two—Ragland-castle, Monmouth; and St. Augustin's Gate, Canterbury, by V. Green

FOREIGNERS.

V

86 Eight—Jean du Verges, by Morin; Ben Varchi, Vin. Viviani, &c.

87 Four—Francois de Vandosme, by Nantueil; Duchesse de la Valiere, N. Marquis de Villeroy, by Morin; and Vaumoricre, by Thomassin

88 Two—F. Duc de Villeroy, by Edelinck, &c.
89 Seven—Pope Urban, &c.
90 One—FRANCISUS VALDESIUS, by Corn. Vifcher—*fine and fcarce*
91 Six—Marfhal Villars, &c.
92 Four—Raphael, by Freij; Paul Veronefe, Anton. Vitre, by Morin; and Anton. Vivaldi, by F. M. la Cave

ENGLISH ENGRAVED PORTRAITS.

V

93 Four—Lord and Lady Vaux, &c. by Dalton, &c.
94 Five—Sir George Vandeput, Dr. de Valengin, by Collyer; P. Vignau, by Gordiner; Henry Voguell, by G. F. Schmidt, 1746; and John Urry, 1714, by N. Pigne
95 Four—Lud. Vives, G. J. Voffius, by A. Blooteling; Adol. Vcrftius, by P. Pontius; and Count Ulfield, &c.
96 Five—Vefalii, Adol. Vorftius, by P. Pontius, &c.
97 One—Sir Thomas Urquhart, fmall whole length, by G. Glover, 1645—*fine and rare*
98 One—ditto, by ditto, 1641, with the copy

ENGLISH MEZZOTINTO PORTRAITS.

V

99 One—Admiral Sir Edward Vernon, whole length, by J. Jones

100 Two—Sir Thomas de Veil, by Ryley—*proof*; and Henry Voguell, 1746, by Faber

101 Two—Admiral Edward Vernon, after Gainſborough, by M'Ardell; and one, by Faber, 1746

Eighteenth Day's Sale.

VANDYCK.

1 FOUR—artifts—Barbe, Van Baelen, Brouer, &c.
2 Seven—artifts—Callot, Cofter, Crayer, &c.
3 Four—artifts—Ertvelt, Vanden Enden, &c.
4 Four—Th. Galle, Vander Geeft, Gentilefci, &c.
5 Six—W. Hondius, Honthorft, P. de Jode, Jordans, and Inigo Jones, by Hollar
6 Three—John Livens; Mirevelt, *a proof*; and Momper
7 Five—Lamen, Mallery, Meiffens, Mildor, and Mytens
8 Four—Palamedes, Pepyn, Poelenbourgh, and P. Pontius
9 Four—Revefteyn, Rombouts, Rubens, and Martin Rychart
10 Four—Segars, Schut, Sachleven, and Snyders
11 Four—Snayers, Stalbert, Steenwyck, and Stevens
12 Four—Vandyck, the buft; Lucas Vorfterman, Corn. de Vos, and Simon Vouet

13 Seven—Vandyck, Vanlonius, Voerst, Vranck, Van Uden, Wildens, and Wolfart

14 Five—portraits of painters, etched by Vandyck

15 Six—ditto

16 Twelve—half lengths, by Lombardt

17 Five—Gus. Adolphus, Count Aremberg on horseback, &c. &c.

18 Five—Earl of Arundel, and Alathea Talbot, by Vorsterman; one by Tardieu, &c.

19 Three—Thomas, Earl of Arundel, by Vorsterman; ditto, and Alathea Talbot, and the Arundel family, small

20 Two—George, Duke of Buckingham, and his brother, 1636; and John and Lord Bernard Stuart, by M'Ardell—*fine*

21 Two—Mich. Le Blon, by Matham; and Christian, Duke of Brunswick—*proof*

22 Seven—Don Alvor Bazau; Cardinal Bentivolus, by Morin; Henry, Count Van Berghe, by Pontius, &c. &c.

23 Five—Count Van Berghe, by Pontius; Couut Bramteville, Johannes de Blois, &c.

24 Two—Charles I. and Henrietta Maria, by Suyderhoef, with rich ornamental borders—*fine*

25 One—ditto, in an oval, hat and cloak, View of London, encircled with two dragons, six Dutch verses, by J. Zoet—*very rare and fine*

26 Two—ditto, on horseback, and the Duke d'Espernon; and ditto, with the Queen, &c. by Baron, 1741

27 Two—Charles I. and the Duke d'Espernon, by Baron, 1741, with the etching—*very scarce*

28 Three—Charles I. in armour, whole length, by P. Gunst; ditto, with Queen and two children, oblong, mez. octavo, and the three children, by Sir Robert Strange

29 One—Charles I. by Vorsterman—*very fine*

30 Three—ditto, right hand on a crown, by Meysens; the etching of ditto, *curious*; and Henrietta Maria, by Joseph Couchet

31 Five—ditto, by R. White, a sheet; ditto, by de Jode, octavo; one ditto, by J. Becket; one ditto, by J. Smith, folio; and one, the same, quarto

32 Three—Charles, Count Palatine, by Bernard, 1657; Charles, de Columna, by Pontius, VANDEN ENDEN; and Charles II. when young, by Hollar

33 One—Charles I. whole length, in his robes, by Sir Robert Strange—*fine*

34 Two—the children of ditto, by ditto; and one ditto, by Richard Cooper, 1762

35 One—ditto, with the Queen, and his children, by Joan Massard, 1784, large sheet—*fine*

36 Two—Charles I. and Henrietta Maria, by P. de Jode, large half sheet—*very fine*

37 Four—Ann, Countess of Caernarvon, by Morin; Lucy, Countess Carlisle, by P. Baillie; ditto, by Gunst, &c.

38 One—Oliver Cromwell, on horseback, by P. Lombart —*fine and scarce*

39 One—Henry, Earl of Danby, whole length, by V. Green—*fine*

40 Four—Lucy, Countess of Carlisle, by Gunst; Sir Kenelm Digby, by V. Voerst; ditto, by Houbraken; and Edward, Earl of Dorset, by M. Vander Gucht

41 Five—Ferdinand of Auſtria, different

*41 Five—Ferdinand III. Roman Emperor; Albert, Duke Fritland, &c.

42 One—Sir Belthazar Gerbier, and family, by W. Walker —*fine proof, ſcarce*

*42 One—ditto, *ditto*

43 Three—James, Duke of Hamilton, in armour, collar of the Garter, by V. Liſebetius; ditto, left hand on a truncheon; ditto, octavo

*43 One—Henrietta Maria, with the Prince of Wales and Duke of York, by Sir Robert Strange, 1784—*fine*

44 Two—Henrietta Maria, by Gunſt; ditto, by P. de Jode, octavo

45 Two—James, Duke of Hamilton, by V. Liſebetius; and HENRY, EARL OF HOLLAND, by Clowet—PROOF

46 One—Henrietta Maria, by George Glover, 1640—*fine and rare*

47 Two—Henrietta Maria, and Charles I. by P. de Jode—*very fine*

48 One—ditto, by De Jode—FINE PROOF

49 One—George, Marquis of Huntly, whole length, by V. Green—*fine*

50 Six—Conſtan. Hugens, Paul Halmalius, &c.

51 Three—Iſabella Clara Eugenia, by V. Sompel; ditto, by Vorſterman; and ditto, by W. Hondius, 1633

52 One—Madam Ann Kirk, whole length, by Becket—*fine*

53 Seven—Juſtus Lipſius, Martin Vanden Enden; Fred. de Marſelaer, John de Montfort, &c.

54 Four—Marg. Lemon, by Morin; Count Mansfield, by Voerſt; Maria de Medicis, by Marten Vanden

Enden; and Maria, daughter of Charles I. by P. de Jode, octavo

55 Seven—Mary of Austria, by Galle; Moncade, by Suyderhoef; ditto, by Vorsterman, &c.

56 One—the Nassau family, by Baron, 1761—*first impression, fine*

57 Two—Frederic Henry, Prince of Orange, by P. Pontius; ditto, by Waumars

58 Five—John, Count Nassau, by Pontius; ditto, by Suyderhoef; ditto, by Vorsterman; and two of Emilia, Princess of Orange

59 One—the Pembroke family, by Baron, 1740

60 Six—Philip IV. on horseback, by P. de Jode; Henry, Count Papeenheim, by C. Galle, &c.

61 Three—William, Duke of Newcastle, by Vertue; N. F de Peirese, by L. Vorsterman; and Philip, Earl Pembroke, by R. Van Voerst

62 Three—James, Duke of Richmond, whole length, by Earlom—*fine*, *proof*; ditto, by Houbraken; and a ditto, octavo

63 Three—Theo. Rogiers, by Clouet; Rubens and Vandyck, in one sheet, by P. Pontius; and Prince Rupert, by H. Snyers

64 Three—Lords John and Bernard Stuart, by R. Tompson; one ditto, by McArdell; and Madam Smith, by Vaillant

65 Five—Alexander Seagia, by Mart. Vanden Enden; A Spinola, by Soutman; Quin Simons, &c.

66 Four—Thomas, Earl of Strafford, by R. White; ditto, by Hollar, 1640; ditto, by Houbraken; ditto, and his secretary, by Vertue

67 One—Rachael, Countefs of Southampton, by M'Ardell—*fine*, *proof*

68 One—Titian and his miftrefs, etched by Vandyck

69 One—ditto—*very fine*

70 Six—Spinola, Dio Tulden, Count Tferclaes, Anton de Taffis, &c.

71 Four—Vandyck, by Carlo Faucci; S. Vouet, by Morin; R—, Earl of Warwick, by Houbraken; and Ann Wake, by Clowet

72 Two—Baron Wandesford, by J. Watfon; and Sir Thomas Wharton, whole length, by V. Green

73 One—COUNTESS OF WARWICK, by Pontius, fmall oval—*proof*, *very rare*

74 Five—Wolf, Count Palatine, Baro Wemmelius, &c.

75 Six—various

76 Ten—The Wharton Family, &c. whole lengths, by Gunft—*fine old impreffion*

VERTUE'S WORKS.

77 One—the Arundel family, after Vandyck—*fine and fcarce*

78 Three—Queen Anne, folio, with medals; and David Bruce, æt. 15, 1710, large fheet, &c.

79 Four—Sir F. Bacon, in an oval; L. Blackburne, 1727; Lord A. Beauclerc, 1740, *proofs*; and Sir John Blencowe, 1713

80 Six—Bagford, 1728; J. Barwick, S. T. P.; A Blackwell; R. Boyle, quarto, 1738; W. Broome, æt. 36, 1726; and John, Duke of Buckingham, quarto, 1722

81 Nine—King Charles I. and the Loyalifts, with the biographical account

82 Five—Cranmer, in an oval, *proof*; two of Chandler, 1738, *one a proof*; J. W. Dawes, octavo; and P. Doddridge, 1751

83 Six—Queen Caroline, fitting, *a proof*; ditto, when Princefs of Wales, large, 1724; Caftiglioni; Wm. Croft; H. Cortes; and William, Duke of Cumberland, quarto

84 Four—Sir Lau. Carter, 1733; Samuel Dale, 1737; Thos. Earl of Dorfet, 1608, and Lionel, Duke of Dorfet, 1732

85 One—EDWARD ELLIOT, of Port-Elliot, and family, 1726—ON INDIA PAPER, SCARCE

86 Two—Edward VI. granting the charter of Bridewell; and Queen Elizabeth's proceffion to Hunfdon-houfe

87 Four—Edward III. and IV. Elizabeth, and Sir Robert Eyre

88 Five—Prince Frederic, *proof*; John Flamftead, 1719; John, Lord Fortefcue, 1747; John Freeke, 1717; and T. Fuller, M. D.

89 Five—John Gale, octavo, *proof*; J. Gilbert; John Gill, folio, 1748; Am. Godfrey, a buft; and Sir Thomas Grefham

90 Five—John Gilbert; Hum. Gower, *proof*; Richard Graves, æt. 59; John Graves, æt. 103, 1728; and Sir Thomas Grefham, *proof*

91 Five—George I. 1714; George, Prince of Wales, 1724; H. Duke of Gloucefter; Lady Jane Grey, and the Familia Regia

92 Two—Familia Regia; and Charles, Earl of Halifax, 1716

93 Six—Sir Matt. Hale; Ant. Hall; Marg. Halyburton, 1747; Edward Harley, 1751; Eliz. Haywood and George Holmes, 1743

94 Five—Sir Matt. Hale; Thomas Harley; Edward Harley, 1751; Sir Edward Harley, 1660; and Benjamin Hoadley

95 Five—Ben Johnſon, folio, *proof*; ditto, octavo; Sir Joſeph Jekyll; Thomas Kenn, octavo; and Sir P. King, oval, 1724

96 Three—John Kenrick, æt. 29; Wm. Lambard, 1601, *proof*; and John Lydgate

97 Five—William Lambard, quarto; William Lanceſter, *proof*; Biſhop Lloyd, æt. 86, 1713; John Locke, octavo; and William Lupton

98 Three—Mary I. after A. More; and two, different, of Mary Queen of Scots

99 Four—Mary Queen of Scots; Milton, æt. 21; ditto, æt. 66, *proof*; and Biſhop Morley

100 One—Sir Hugh Myddleton—FINE AND SCARCE

101 Six—Walter Moyle, æt. 49, 1721; F. Mundy, æt. 29, 1720; John Murray, *proof*; Sir Iſaac Newton, æt. 83; Robert, Earl of Orford; and the Hon. Counteſs of Orrery, 1732

102 Eight—Sir F. Page, 1720; Daniel Parke, 1710; Matt. Parker, in an oval; Philip V.; John Potter, 1737; Matt. Prior, 1719; James Puckle; and Father Paul

103 Four—Sir F. Page, 1720; Henry Powle, 1737; Sir Robert Raymond, 1724; and James Reynolds, 1730

104 Four—Racine, quarto; Sir Walter Raleigh; Sir Thomas Rawlinſon, Lord Mayor, 1706; and John Robinſon, organiſt

105 Four—Biſhops—John Robinſon, of Briſtol; James Sharp, of St. Andrew's; Richard Smalbroke, of Litchfield, 1733; and George Smalridge, of Briſtol, 1724

106 Six—George Smallridge; Robert South; John Spencer, 1727; Spinckes, 1727; Joſeph Stennet, and Jonathan Swift, in an oval, folio

Nineteenth Day's Sale.

FOREIGNERS.

W

1 FIVE—William VI. of Heſſe-Caſſel; William VIII. of ditto, by Houbraken; Koningſmark, Count Weſterwick, by Falck, 1651, &c.

2 One—Corn. and John de Witt, with their execution at the bottom

3 Three—Corn. and John de Witt, in the middle of ſixteen hiſtorical compartments, by R. de Hooge, John de Witt, by J. Barry, and Corn. de Witt, by Capt. Baillie

4 Six—Four portraits of Corn. and John de Witt, and two of their executions

5 Eight—various, after Titian, Guido, &c.

6 Five—Xaverius, by Vermeulen, &c.

VERTUE'S CONTINUED.

7 Five—Eliz. Counteſs of Shrewſbury; Sir Phil. Sidney, *proofs*; Thomas, Earl of Stafford, after Vandyck; Children of ditto; and Thomas, Earl of ditto, 1714

8 Five—William, Duke of Somerſet, 1671; Sir James Steuart, æt. 78; Thomas, Earl of Strafford; and ditto, 1714

9 Four—Sir Philip Sidney, ditto, *proof*; Sir John Suckling; and Henry Earl of Surrey, ob. 1546

10 Five—Rad. Taylor, æt. 75, 1722; Edward Teniſon, Biſhop of Oſſory, 1731; J. Thurloo, William Trumbull, and Daniel Turner

11 Two—William Trumbull, and Sir WILLIAM TRUMBULL—*proof*, *ſcarce*

12 Six—Thomas Vernon, 1725; Edmund Waller, folio; William Peere Williams, 1740; Sir Ralph Winwood; Wollaſton, quarto; and Sir Watkin William Wynn, 1742

13 Three—P. Verignon, 1722; William Whiſton, 1720; and the Pope's Tiara

14 Three—Uſher; John Weſley; and Biſhop Wilſon, of Man, 1726

ENGLISH MEZZOTINTO PORTRAITS.

W

15 Three—Thomas Walker, actor, by Faber, 1728; Mr. Thomas Wright, by Frye, 1737; and Sir Benj. Wrench, M. D. æt. 82, 1747

Y

16 Three—General Wade, in oval, by Faber, 1736; Colonel Thomas Wentworth, by Van Haecken; and General Wills, by J. Simon

17 Two—General Wade, by Vanacken, 1736; and Sir James Wiſhart, by Faber, 1722

18 Four—Gen. Wade, by Vanhaecken; Admiral Sir Peter Warren, 1751, by Faber; Charles Watſon, by E. Fiſher; and Captain Andrew Wilkinſon, by H. Hudſon

19 Two—Admiral Sir Charles Wager, 1726, by G. White; and the etching—*ſcarce*

20 One—George, Prince of Wales; and Prince Frederick, Biſhop of Oſnaburg, after Weſt, by V. Green—*proof*

21 One—George, Prince of Wales, ſtanding with his horſe, after Gainſborough, by J. R. Smith—*proof*

22 Three—Sir Robert Walpole, whole length, 1741, by Faber; ditto, in oval, by Simon; and ditto, with Fortitude, Juſtice, &c. by Sympſon

23 Two—Sir Robert Walpole, in an oval, by G. White, 1715; and Mrs. Catherine Walpole, by Simon—*fine*

24 One—Sir Robert Walpole, whole length, by Faber—*fine proof*

25 One—Baron Wandesford, after Vandyck, by James Watſon

26 Two—Generals Waſhington and Green, whole length, after Peele, by V. Green—*proofs*, *ſcarce*

27 Three—Waſhington, in a ſquare, after Trumbull, by V. Green—*proof*, and two cut ones

28 One—ditto, after ditto, 1780, whole length, by Val. Green

29 Two—Guſtavus Waltz, by J. S. Miller; and Maſter Samuel Weſley, by W. Dickenſon, whole length

30 One—GEORGE WELD, OF WILLEY, in the county of Salop, Esq. deputy-lieutenant of the Tower of London, in the 15th year of the reign of King Charles II.—VERY RARE—NOT IN BROMLEY.

31 Two—Benj. West and Son, 1773; and Mrs. West and Son, by V. Green—*proofs*

32 Four—Philip, Duke of Wharton, by Simon; Thomas, Marquis ditto, by ditto; John Wilkes, by Ritcheman; and William Wollaston, quarto, by Faber

33 One—William Wilberforce, M. P. by C. H. Hodges, 1791—*proof*

34 One—William III. on horseback, at the battle of Namur, 1695, after Wyck, by Faber, 1743

35 Two—William and Mary, by Verkolye—*the king a proof*

36 Two—William and Mary, in their robes, whole length, by B. Lens—*very fine*

37 Four—William, on horseback, a ditto, in an oval, by G. Valck; a ditto, by R. Williams, &c.

38 Two—Master and Miss Williams, after Wright, by V. Green—*proof*; and Miss Stuart, ditto

39 Three—John Wilkes, by James Watson, a toping meeting between a parson, a steward, and a poet, Van Goucht, del. et sculp. and James Worsdale, by W. Dickenson

40 One—Sir Armine Woodehouse, by Charles Townley, 1772—*scarce*

41 One—Mr. Philip Woollrich, by F. Place—*very fine and rare*

42 Two—Arthur Wentworth, by V. Green, and William Woodfall—*proofs*

CLERGY.

43 Three—Bifhops—Stephen Wefton, of Exeter, 1731, by G. White; Willes, of Bath, &c. 1743, by Faber; and Richard Willes, of Gloucefter, by J. Simon

44 Three—Thomas Walker, L.L.D. 1728; W. Warren, L.L.D. by W. Robins, 1731; and Stephen Wefton, by G. White

45 Two—George Walker—*a proof*; James Warner, V.D.M. in an ornamented oval

46 Two—Mr. Wallen, by P. Borgnis—*a proof*; and George Whitefield, whole length, by James Watfon

ENGLISH ENGRAVED PORTRAITS.

W

47 Ten—various; Jofeph Warder, Wafhington, George Wilfon, Woodward, &c.

48 Five—The children of Count Woronzor, by Caroline Watfon, &c.

49 Five—Thomas Walker, L. L. D. 1764; Sir Edward Ward, by R. White, 1702; Sir Chriftopher Wray, 1582, by Harding; Sir Robert Wright, by R. White, &c.

50 Three—Writing-mafters; Thomas Wefton, by R. White; Eleazer Wigan, 1695, by J. Sturt; and a fheet of fix, by Bickham

51 Five—Watteau and his brother; one the etching; Worlidge, by himſelf—*on ſattin*, &c.

52 Four—Sir Robert Walpole; Sir Watkin William Wynne, by Aberry, 1753; a ditto, by B. Wilſon; and Thomas, Marquis of Wharton, by Houbraken

53 Four—Edward Waterhouſe, 1663, by D. Loggan; William Walwyn, æt. 80, by R. White; Thomas Willis, M. D. æt. 45, by D. Loggan; and Thomas Willsford, æt. 46, by R. Vaughan

54 Five—Edward Waterhouſe, by A. Hertochs; Sir F. Walſingham, &c.

55 Twelve—Portraits to illuſtrate Granger, &c.

56 Six—Lord Wentworth; Thomas Wiatt, &c. by Dalton, &c.

57 Four—Lady Warner, by P. Vanſchuppen, 1690; Mary, Counteſs of Warwick, 1678, by R. White; Richard Whittington, by R. Elſtrache; and Sir Hen. Wotton, folio

58 Eight—Waller, by Vanderbanc; Whittington, &c.

59 Eight—Lady Warner; Mary, Counteſs of Warwick; Sir George Wharton, by Croſs, ſix Engliſh verſes; ditto, by Chantry, ditto; Withers, by Payne; John Woodhull, by G. Glover, &c.

60 Three—Sir William Waller; Lord Willoughby, of Parham; and Edward, Earl of Worceſter, by Simon Paſſe

41 One—William, Viscount Wallingford—extra fine and rare

62 One—Robert Walker, by Lombart—*fine ana ſcarce*

63 One—William Wattſon, of Stower, in Dorſet, M. D. by R. Parr—*rare*

64 One—Sir John Webster, eight Latin lines, by T. Matham—*first impression, very rare*

65 One—DITTO—*a paoof, extra rare*

66 Two—Darcy Wentworth, 1624, by W. Passe—*scarce*; and the copy

67 One—MILDMAY, EARL OF WESTMORELAND, by P. Williamson, 1662—*fine and rare*

68 One—Bulstrode Whitelock, in an oval, by R. Gaywood—*rare*

69 One—Thomas Whithorn, wood cut, from "his" contra Tenor, 1571—*rare*

70 One—Mr. Justice Willes, by James Heath, after T. Gainsborough

71 Seven—William III. various

72 One—SIR FRANCIS WINDERBANK AND LORD FINCH, WITH FINCH'S WINGS FLYING TO WINDYBANK——*extra rare*

CLERGY.

73 Seven—G. A. Wachsel, by J. Miller; John Wesley, hand on a book; Stephen Whisson, by Trotter, 1784; Thomas Wills; Elh. Winchester, by Robinson, 1792; John Witherspoon, by Trotter; and F. M. Ziegenhægen, by G. H. Smith

74 Fourteen—various; Luther, Calvin, &c.

75 Five—George Walker, by A. Haelweg; Thomas Waterhonse; Richard Walton, octavo, &c.

76 Two—William Wake, by M. Vandregucht; and Brian Walton, æt. 57, 1657, by Lombart

77 Three—George Walker, by P. Vandrebanc, 1689, before the addreſs of the publiſher; B. Walton, by Lombart; and Richard Walton, folio

78 One—JOHN WALLIS, by D. Loggan—PROOF

79 Two—ditto, by D. Loggan; and one by M. Burghers, 1699

80 Three—William Walker, æt. 59, quarto; Thomas Watſon, by Sturt, folio; George Webb, of Limerick, by Slater

81 Four—W. Whatelie, æt. 58, ſix Latin lines; William Whitacres, by W. Marſhall; John White, S. T. P. ſix Latin verſes; Francis White, æt. 59, by Cockſon

82 Two—Biſhop George Webb; and Thomas Wilſon, ſix Engliſh verſes, both by Croſs—*fine*

83 Three—Daniel Whitby, S. T. P. æt. 71, by M. Vandregucht; Francis White, by G. Mountaine, ſix Latin verſes; and An. Willett, with ſix Latin verſes, folio—*fine*

84 Five—Henry Wharton, by R. White, octavo; Ben. Whichcot, ditto; Jeremiah White, æt. 78, 1707; Eras. Williams, æt. 56, 1608—*a monumental plate*; and Thomas Wiſe, by M. Vandregucht, octavo

85 Three—Biſhop John Wilkins, of Cheſter, by A. Blooteling; John Williams, Biſhop of Lincoln, in a hat, ſold by Jenner; and Cardinal Wolſey, 1629, quarto

86 Three—Thomas Wilſon, Biſhop of Man, by J. and C. Sherwin—*proof*; a ditto, by Trotter; and a ditto, æt. 90, by J. Nouel, 1752, folio

ENGLISH MEZZOTINTO PORTRAITS.

Y

87 One—Mrs. Yates, as Melpomene, after Romney, by V. Green—*proof*

88 One—Frederick, Duke of York, whole length, in his uniform, after Hopner, by C. H. Hodges—*proof*

89 Two—James, Duke of York, by Verkoljé; and Maria, Duchefs of York, by R. Williams, in ovals

90 Two—Mrs. Agneta Yorke; boy and dog, by V. Green—*proofs*

91 Two—the Hon. Sidney Yorke; and Mrs. Agneta Yorke, ditto—*ditto*

ENGLISH ENGRAVED PORTRAITS

Y

92 Three—Mr. Yeates, in the character of Launce, by H. Roberts; John Yenn, architect, by J. K. Sherwin; P. P. and William Young, by Holloway

93 One—Robert, Earl of Yarmouth, by P. Vandrebranc, a fheet

94 Three—James, Duke of York, by R. White; ditto, whole length, by Loggan; and Mary, Duchefs of ditto, by Vandrebanc

95 Three—James, Duke of York, by R. White; Anne, Duchefs of ditto, by Lombart, 1669; and one, by Simonneau

96 One—James, Duke of York, in armour, trophies, &c. by R. White, 1682, a ſheet—*fine*

97 One—ditto, by Van Dalen

98 A parcel, various

99 A ditto

BOOKS OF PRINTS AND PORTFOLIOS.

100 Strutt's Dreſſes, eight numbers

101 A ſet of portraits to Sir John Hawkens's Hiſtory of Muſic

102 Sixteen, Thane's autographs, vol. ii.

103 Vertue's head, medals, and monuments, of the kings of England—*large paper uncut, a fine ſet*

104 Houbraken's heads, ditto, not complete

105 Holben's Court of Henry VIII. 36 portraits, by Dalton

106 Heads and views to Harding's Shakeſpeare—wants three heads

107 A ſet of Emperors and Popes

108 A portfolio of the beſt ſtout vellum paper, bound in Ruſſia, 33 inches by 26

109 A ditto, 28 by 21, lettered; Granger's Britiſh Biography, vol. iii

110 A ditto, ditto, vol. iv

☞ Immediately after, will be ſold the Collection of Gold, Silver, and Copper, Coins and Medals; due Notice will be given.

THE END.